English Literature

Values and Traditions

Benjamin Ifor Evans

Routledge
Taylor & Francis Group
Routledge Revivals

First published in 1962
by Routledge & Kegan Paul

This edition first published in 2018 by Routledge
2 Park Square, Milton Park, Abingdon, Oxon, OX14 4RN
and by Routledge
711 Third Avenue, New York, NY 10017

Routledge is an imprint of the Taylor & Francis Group, an informa business

Publisher's Note
The publisher has gone to great lengths to ensure the quality of this reprint but points out that some imperfections in the original copies may be apparent.

Disclaimer
The publisher has made every effort to trace copyright holders and welcomes correspondence from those they have been unable to contact.
A Library of Congress record exists under ISBN: 62053248

ISBN 13: 978-1-138-50110-2 (hbk)
ISBN 13: 978-1-315-14418-4 (ebk)
ISBN 13: 978-1-138-50117-1 (pbk)

Routledge Revivals

English Literature

First published in 1962, this book is a reflection on Sir Ifor Evans's well-known *A Short History of English Literature*. In this reflective study, Evans wonders if it is possible to trace permanent elements in such a huge and varied mass of writings? As he moves from the Anglo-Saxon Caedmon to T.S Eliot, or from Milton to James Joyce, he finds out how, in unexpected ways, the English spirit of compromise extends into its literature, along with its love of nature and interest in the individual. In poetic imagery above all the British genius seems, typically, to have found a way of making 'empiricism transcendental'. This book, which had its origin during the war under the aegis of the British Council, provides the reader with a stimulating passport to a very rich kingdom.

ENGLISH LITERATURE:

VALUES AND TRADITIONS

In his well-known book *A Short History of English Literature*, Sir Ifor Evans described and defined his subject; here he reflects on it. Is it possible, he wonders, to trace permanent elements in such a huge and varied mass of writings? As he moves from the Anglo-Saxon Caedmon to T. S. Eliot, or from Milton to James Joyce, he finds how, in unexpected ways, the English spirit of compromise extends into her literature, along with her love of nature and interest in the individual. In poetic imagery above all the British genius seems, typically, to have found a way of making 'empiricism transcendental'. This book which had its origin during the war under the aegis of the British Council, provides the reader with a stimulating passport to a very rich kingdom.

By the same Author

Criticism and Biography

TRADITION AND ROMANTICISM

ENGLISH POETRY IN THE LATER NINETEENTH CENTURY

KEATS

THE POETRY OF WILLIAM MORRIS

ENGLISH LITERATURE BETWEEN THE WARS

A SHORT HISTORY OF ENGLISH LITERATURE

THE USE OF ENGLISH

SCIENCE AND LITERATURE

Travel

ENCOUNTERS

Fiction

IN SEARCH OF STEPHEN VANE

THE SHOP ON THE KING'S ROAD

THE CHURCH IN THE MARKETS

Edited with W. W. Greg

THE COMEDY OF SUSANNA (*Malone Society*)

JACK JUGGLER (*Malone Society*)

With M. C. Glasgow

THE ARTS IN ENGLAND

SIR IFOR EVANS, D. LIT.

ENGLISH LITERATURE: VALUES AND TRADITIONS

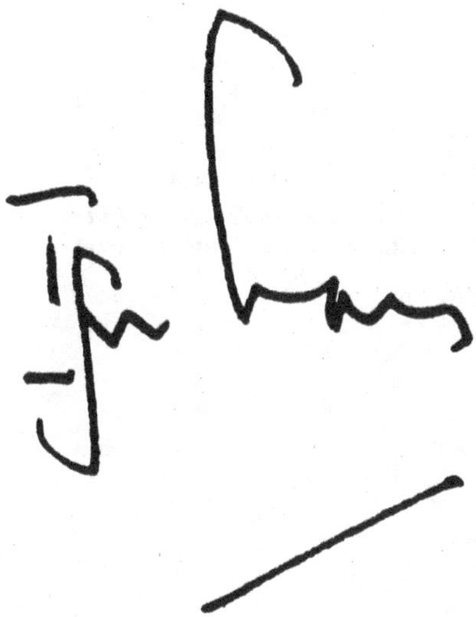

LONDON · UNWIN BOOKS

First Published in this edition 1962

UNWIN BOOKS

George Allen & Unwin Ltd
Ruskin House, Museum Street
London W.C.1

PRINTED IN GREAT BRITAIN
in 10 on 12pt. Plantin type
BY C. TINLING & CO. LTD
LIVERPOOL, LONDON AND PRESCOT

PREFACE

In 1942 I wrote a brief volume on the permanent traditions in English Literature for the British Council. Actually it was written by the courtesy of a Royal Air Force officer in the corner of the dining room of a crowded ship that went from England to Lagos in convoy in September and October of that year.

I discovered that it was still being used after the war, but on re-reading it I was shocked to discover how far one's thinking had been affected by the war atmosphere.

At Sir Stanley Unwin's suggestion I have re-written the text and expanded it. The British Council have kindly allowed me to use as much of the original volume as was still appropriate.

It may be doubted whether one can generalize in this way with any effect. My colleague Professor Gombrich has done so with such brilliance for art that I was led to continue the attempt.

I.E.

I

In 1940 the Cambridge University Press issued one of the most important publications on English literature to appear in England during this century. This was *The Cambridge Bibliography of English Literature* edited by F. W. Bateson. It is not a book that one can read, but to turn its pages is to realize the extent and range of the literature which has been composed in England. Within three of its four massive volumes it contains the record, in chronological order, of 'the authors, titles and editions with relevant critical matter, of all the writings in book-form (whether English or Latin) that can still be said to possess some literary interest, written by English people whether in the United Kingdom or overseas'.

These lists, which exclude everything written in the present century, occupy three thousand and thirteen closely printed pages with two columns on each page. To turn the pages of this bibliography is to realize that books have been composed and written in England for over a thousand years, and, though contrary views on this matter exist, it will be urged later that they belong to one continuous tradition however diverse and variegated. So ample has been the production that even the most diligent reader, blessed with industry and longevity, could not hope to master more than a small part of the contents.

If Mr Bateson and his army of helpers need over three thousand pages to make a list of the items in which English literature is to be found it would obviously be a mockery to attempt a summary of the form and pattern of all that output in a short volume. What is attempted is to see whether there is some continuing tradition, some qualities which make this literature distinct, both in virtues and defects, from that of other countries. As has been already indicated, no single person can read the whole of this literature, so any generalization must be based on a partial view and to some extent on the summaries and findings of others. Yet, it can be maintained, and this without distortion, that there can be discovered in these long-continued and voluminous manifestations certain characteristics recurring from one age to another which give to all parts of English literature a definable quality, even a unity.

II

It is sometimes urged that these permanent or persistent features are ultimately a reflection of English life itself and of the history and society of England. Here one treads on dangerous ground, and all such generalizations deserve to be approached with caution. In no country has more than a minority of the population been interested in the arts. For the greater part of the centuries under survey a large part of the population was illiterate, and what could be obtained by an oral tradition was necessarily very limited.

No literary work has had the influence of the major religious books of the world: the Bible, the Koran and the Vedas have obviously influenced men's lives and behaviour in a way incomparable to the most popular literary work of a secular kind. In Christendom this is true despite the fact that in the great ages of the faith, the vast populations of Christians were unable to read the text of the Bible, for from the early centuries of the Church it was one version or other of the much revised Vulgate or Latin Bible that was in circulation. In England there had very early been a natural longing for a vernacular rendering: Caedmon (flourished about 670) according to Bede an 'unlettered herdsman' had rendered parts of the Scriptures into verse in the seventh century, and Bede himself (died 735) translated the Gospel of St John. Before Wyclif's death in 1384 the whole of the Bible had been translated accurately even if clumsily. Finally in 1611 the Authorized Version appeared, based on the work of over a hundred men, mainly of the Tudor period, and whose renderings were incorporated by a committee into moving and dignified Jacobean prose. Outstanding among the earlier versions had been that of

William Tyndale (from 1525) and Miles Coverdale (from 1535). The Authorized version by the beauty of its style entered permanently into the tradition of English prose.

Next to these sacred works some political writers have had a far greater influence upon men's lives than works of imagination. Even Thomas Paine (1737-1809), the English revolutionary writer, had a profound effect in America with his *Common Sense* (1776) which urged immediate and unrestricted independence in a way with which imaginative writers cannot compete. Further, to quote a work composed in England but written in German, *Das Kapital* (first volume appeared in 1867) of Karl Marx ultimately changed not only political philosophy and the writing of history but the shape of history itself.

Though the matter can easily be exaggerated, the size of the audience for literature was limited before William Caxton (1422-91) set up his press at Westminster in 1476. Caxton printed *The Canterbury Tales* and *Troilus and Criseyde*, but before that time these great poems by Chaucer had to be read to audiences except for the lucky few who had a manuscript copied by a scrivener.[1] Nor did the conditions of the time allow for full-time professional authorship, except under the protection of the Church. Further, until the sixteenth century the limitation of travel and the absence of any national unity led to great variations in language from one part of the kingdom to the other. Chaucer at the conclusion of *Troilus and Criseyde* had written of 'the great diversity in English and in the writing of our tongue', while Caxton in a well known passage speaks of the variation of English from one shire to another. He describes how a man who asked for 'eggs' had no satisfaction until it was explained that they were 'eyren' and he adds, 'Lo, what should a man these days now write, *eggs* or *eyren*? Certainly it is hard to please every man by cause of diversity

[1]See *Chaucer and the Fifteenth Century*, H. S. Bennett, 1947.

and change of language'. In the fifteenth century literacy increased: it was no longer the perquisite of clerics and learned men but often an accomplishment of country gentlemen and their wives.

One of the miracles of English literature is the degree to which conditions had improved in little more than a century after Caxton's death. Though the assessment can be little more than an intelligent guess, the population of England in the time of Elizabeth I was 5,000,000. Many of these were still illiterate, yet there was in London above all, but also in a number of provincial centres, a growing number of people who could read.

Apart from the censorship of books to which reference is made later,[1] it had become possible for a professional writer to make a living, some sort of a living, from the booksellers. There was a court which delighted in literature and a Queen who was herself a mistress of style. Indeed it could be said that at no period had literature such a direct effect on the life of the country. The Virgin Queen, though political considerations made her wary in taking a suitor, encouraged a romantic adoration of her person, especially in verse. 'This cult', as Professor Hurstfield writes,[2] 'has never been properly investigated. When it is, it will no doubt call for other approaches besides that of the historian. Ultimately a study of this kind may well open up a new vision of Elizabethan government and society. This is not to say that Elizabeth invented the cult; nor that it was invented and fostered by any particular group of men: nor that the adulation in which Elizabeth basked was insincere. What, however, can be said is that, in this process of deification Elizabeth found to hand a political instrument of immense power, subtlety and range, and that she used it with consummate skill, wisdom, courage and ingenuity'. Fortunately

[1]Page 35.
[2]*Elizabeth I and the Unity of England*, J. Hurstfield, 1960.

she had great poets to fulfil these purposes. When Edmund Spenser (1552-1599) addressed his *Faerie Queene*, 'To the Most High, Mighty and Magnificent Empress' he knew that the Royal Lady would read his poem. Fortunately it was at such a time that William Shakespeare (1564-1616) wrote. Whatever the antagonism of the Puritans to the theatre and the stresses of the censorship imposed by officialdom Shakespeare had an audience in the court, and at its centre the admiration of the Queen. As is suggested later, he had also the genius of appealing at the same time to the centres of courtly elegance and to auditors of a humble character.

Possibly the author was never in such a central and influential place as in those early Elizabethan days, when writers of genius were touched by the 'buoyancy' of the young nationhood. 'It was in 1575 that the tide of prosperity really turned and it flowed for another decade in England's favour . . . and, a decade later, Christopher Marlowe (1564-1593) would sing his praise of the eager years of English thought and culture, of

> Our souls whose faculties can comprehend
> The wondrous architecture of the world,
> And measure every wandering planet's course
> Still climbing after knowledge infinite.'[1]

By the end of Elizabeth's reign disenchantment had broken in, and so it was to continue under the Stuarts. The effect on literature was to make it amorphous, and sectionalised. Often the author was consciously addressing a minority audience. Milton in the seventeenth century and Johnson in the eighteenth were not fully intelligible except to those who had some acquaintance with the classics. The concept of a society all literate, and all anxious for the excitement of learning and the imagina-

[1]Professor Hurstfield, *loc cit.*

tion was altogether strange to them, as it would have been to their contemporaries in any European country.

It was in the nineteenth century that in England this hope of a fully literate nation, capable of exercising its mind in learning and the arts began to develop in the more optimistic of Liberal circles. Yet education as far as it extended, even modestly, to the elements of reading and writing was not made compulsory in England until the Forster Act of 1870. When the vast generation of new readers thus created grew to be adults they found the old minority literature of the past centuries but little to their taste. They fed themselves on the 'new' journalism of Alfred Harmsworth (later Lord Northcliffe) and the facile, anecdotal, 'tit-bit', periodicals that he and his contemporaries created. One to benefit from these changes in values was Robert Louis Stevenson (1850-94) when in 1883 his *Treasure Island*, intended as a boys' serial, proved to be popular with the new literature adults. No artist has yet appeared able to bridge this great gap between the minority who have had the education and the taste to make the enjoyment of literature almost a necessity of life and the vast audience, now no longer illiterate, but still no part of a book-reading public.

As is suggested later, Shakespeare under the most complex conditions had a certain success with a multiple audience. In the nineteenth century the nearest approach to this universality was attained by Charles Dickens (1812-70) from the moment when without publicity or advertisement *Pickwick Papers* began to sell forty thousand copies of every number. He penetrated to a large audience, which did not normally read books, though probably, unlike Shakespeare, his influence in sophisticated circles was limited. He was a radical and a reformer apart from being a great imaginative writer and a supreme entertainer, but no longer could a writer speak to all sections of England, for the country itself was too divided. Disraeli had spoken of the 'two nations' and Dickens, on the whole, spoke more to the vast audience of the unprivileged and dispossessed, than to the small wealthy society that owned and controlled the country. Further in Dickens's day there was still a considerable element that could not read.

Thus all generalizations from literature to national life must recognize this place of the arts as a minority activity, and one whose importance writers are ever likely to over-estimate. Yet one must not on the other hand carry this argument too far. The writer though belonging to a minority group is not necessarily writing about the minority. Chaucer, in the fourteenth century, described in *The Canterbury Tales* a whole range of society, and the portraits of the illiterate are as vivid and sympathetic as those of the learned and of gentlefolk. So has it often been in English literature. The writer penetrates beyond his own circle and attempts a wider picture of his country and of his times. It is very difficult to see how Shakespeare, the young man from Stratford-upon-Avon, captured into his plays 'the finer shades' of courtly behaviour. Further it was Thomas Gray the scholar, recluse and the friend of Horace Walpole (1716-71), who in the *Elegy Written in a Country Churchyard* paid the most moving tribute in English verse to the unremembered poor:

Full many a gem of purest ray serene,
The dark unfathom'd caves of ocean bear:
Full many a flower is born to blush unseen,
And waste its sweetness on the desert air.

Some village-Hampden, that with dauntless breast
The little Tyrant of the fields withstood,
Some mute inglorious Milton here may rest,
Some Cromwell guiltless of his country's blood.

It was of this poem that Samuel Johnson, a harsh critic in his appraisal of Gray, commented: 'In the character of his

Elegy I rejoice to concur with the common reader: for by the common sense of readers, uncorrupted with literary prejudices, after all the refinements of subtility and the dogmatism of learning must be finally decided all claim to poetical honours ... Had Gray written often thus, it had been vain to blame, and useless to praise him.'

If however, one proceeds cautiously and with hesitation some relation can be found between literature and the social pattern as a whole, though it must always be recognized that the writer is looking at it all from a privileged point of view, with resources outside the range of the majority of his contemporaries.

III

Mr Bateson's bibliography covered the literature of Great Britain and the Commonwealth. The observations in this volume are based on the literature written in English in Great Britain. This, of course, excludes a great deal. For instance the major part of the literature of Wales is written in Welsh, and belongs not only to a separate tradition but to a different language. Similarly such Scottish writers as have written in Gaelic are omitted. Yet while Welsh, Scottish and Irish writers have each their own independent language and tradition their legends and history have entered largely into English literature. It is difficult to conceive how impoverished English literature would be without the romantic tradition that derives from the Celtic source of the Arthurian legends. These stories were already enriching the poetry of the Middle Ages before the time of Chaucer and they have recurred until the late nineteenth century where they form one of the main themes of Tennyson's poetry. Welsh characters have enlivened English literature, as varied in Shakespeare as the magical and dignified prince Glendower and the brave and impetuous soldier Fluellen. Welsh history and spurious history have fed the imagination since the bold inventions of Geoffrey of Monmouth (1100-1154). It was Geoffrey who made the stories of Arthur 'radiant with poetic colouring' and added them to the imaginative inheritance of Europe. Legends and pseudo-history from this Celtic fringe continue in the eighteenth century to initiate a 'gothic' or romantic invention as in Thomas Gray's *The Bard*.

The most notable contribution of Ireland has been of more recent times despite the temporary popularity in the early nineteenth century of Thomas Moore's (1779-1852) *Irish Melodies* (1807-34). The movement which grew up in Dublin between 1885 and 1895 was definitely organized for Irish freedom and a re-expression of the Irish spirit and a recovery of its myths and legends. Fortunately it attracted men of genius, notably W. B. Yeats (1865-1939) whose poetical strength seemed to derive from some deep and ancient Celtic source. He was to become the greatest poet writing in English in the first half of the twentieth century. From his early romantic poems of an Irish origin, such as *The Wanderings of Oisin* (1889) and romantic dramas such as *The Countess Cathleen* (1892), he developed to the bare, astringent but deeply moving poetry of his later period as in *The Tower* (1928). Irish impulses were often still present, including motives derived from the tragic scenes of contemporary Irish history but the imagination had increased in depth and lucidity until its contrivances were unmatched by anything in the age. In the group in which Yeats had developed there were others who again brought the Irish imagination to English readers. J. M. Synge (1871-1909) with an Irish origin and a French background was quickened to creation by Yeats's suggestion that he should visit the Aran Islands. A series of dramas from *The Shadow of the Glen* (1903) to *The Playboy of the Western World* (1907) followed in quick succession. These and others gave to Ireland at the end of the nineteenth century and in the early twentieth a special place for readers of English literature.

The contribution from Scotland has had even a wider influence, for it has been sustained by two men whose genius has had a very wide appeal. Robert Burns (1759-96) tried to conceal his subtle and well-read mind in the disguise of a simple rustic. He employed a language varying between standard English and his native Ayrshire to compose lyrics and poetical satires of great vigour, sometimes sentimental and sometimes in fierce antagonism to the inequalities imposed on man by man. Such was their quality that they captured the attention of his time and have entered permanently into the literary tradition, particularly of his own native Scotland. Sir Walter Scott (1771-1832) in his wide ranging imagination re-awakened in poems and novels scenes from the Middle Ages to the Scotland of the eighteenth century and this in a way that not only engaged English and Scottish audiences but captured the imagination of Europe and touched men to new literary endeavours in France, Germany and Russia. Nor was it alone from Scottish genius that Scotland had an influence. As with Wales an invented legend and mythology affected the imaginative tradition most powerfully. James Macpherson (1736-96) with his Ossianic prose-poems published in 1760 what were supposed to be *Fragments of Ancient Poetry* 'translated from the Gaelic or Erse' but which were largely his own invention. He alleged that they belonged to the ancient tradition of legend that had found its way from Ireland to Scotland. He consolidated his invention in *Fingal* 1762, and Scotland gladly claimed the invention as a national poem, forgetting to what extent had the origins been genuinely ancient they would have been Irish epic. The high sounding rhetoric of this Ossianic verse made a deep impression on his own generation, and not only in Scotland and England; Napoleon and Goethe were among those who fell under their fabricated spell.

It is difficult to conceive how thin English literature itself would have been without these exciting entanglements with Wales, Scotland and Ireland even though the native literatures of these countries remain an unknown territory to English readers.

In confining this study to English literature in Great Britain it has been further necessary to exclude all that varied and exciting literature which has been written in the United States of America in what was in its origins, basically, the English tongue. That is a separate story and an enthralling one. In the early stages American literature belongs to a colonial tradition, relying in its models and language on England and more generally on Western Europe. Washington Irving, born in 1783, the year when the colonies finally achieved their independence, may be regarded as the first author of the new republic. Yet Irving in his ponderous history and in some of his imaginative work was heavily dependent on England. He broke through to something more genuinely American in his legends of the Hudson River, in *Rip Van Winkle* and *The Legend of Sleepy Hollow*. American fiction had already in the eighteen-twenties gained its own identity of scene in such works as Fenimore Cooper's *The Last of the Mohicans* 1826; with Herman Melville, whose *Moby Dick* was published in 1851, it discovered a romance writer of genius. With Edgar Allen Poe America had a writer in prose and verse who not only had great independent stature in his own country but was a major influence in Western Europe, particularly in France. As a short story writer he had a vogue second only to that of Scott, as a novelist. With Poe American literature had moved far from the early colonial stage and had conquered the English-speaking world. So it has continued. The size of the American public itself, the range of its literary achievement, has made the American language a major medium throughout the world and given very wide circulation to American literature, which has been cunning in exploiting its own national and regional themes. The language has been arresting and original, often lively in a way not unlike Shakespearian language with vivid imagery and adaptations of vocabulary. But this American language is a separate language as American literature is a separate literature. It is a story to be told separately.

Again each of the countries of the Commonwealth has its own literature, and these are not yet sufficiently known in England. Even in countries whose languages of origin have not been English there has developed, as particularly in India, a literature in the English tongue. The same is true, in a lively and interesting way, among young writers in the new countries of Africa. Here all this is excluded and the attempt made solely to consider the permanent elements in English literature alone.

IV

THERE remains a more complex problem of definition in relation to the literature of England itself. For the question of when does English literature begin has long been a theme of discussion, and even sharp dispute among literary historians. The modernists would start English literature with Geoffrey Chaucer (1340-1400), and he is certainly the first Englishman writing in English who has had a world reputation and a continuing audience from his own time to the present day. With his travels and his knowledge of French and Italian he had attained an outlook which was European, and despite his affection for older traditions he was modern in much of his outlook and achievement. If one is prepared to skip some of the words, his verse is in large stretches intelligible even without a translation, and reads, particularly in the *Prologue* and in some of the stories in *The Canterbury Tales*, as a picture of life, so vivid and realistic that the men and women he portrays stand out, identifiable across the centuries as part of a common humanity which is ageless. While it is true that most readers of English literature will not penetrate beyond Chaucer, to begin the history of the literature with him would be to exclude at least seven centuries. In fact, literature had been continuously produced in England for more centuries before Chaucer's death than in the period after he died in 1400.

Much of that literature is as unintelligible today as if it had been written in a foreign language. For most English people it belongs to a lost heritage. Some of it was brought over by the Angles and others when they invaded this country. Or if the poems themselves were made in this country, the stories on which they were based were part of the traditions of the homelands of the intruding warriors. So it is with *Beowulf*, the first poetic epic to survive in this country. The theme belonged to the Angles, and it is set not even in their country but in Scandinavia. It was part of their tradition when they came as invaders in the sixth century, and later about A.D. 700 the story was composed into a poem, though the existing manuscript is about three hundred years later. The story of the monster Grendel who is harrying King Hrothgar of Denmark seems very remote to the modern reader, and the long alliterative line is something strange to an ear accustomed to any of the measures used from Chaucer onwards, and the vocabulary of the 'picture-words' seems strange. Yet with all its grotesqueness *Beowulf* is an epic, a poem of some substance and a picture of a society. Some poems come closer to the readers in our own age and many who know nothing else of this early age have heard of the *Maldon*, written just after the battle, and recall the two lines:

> Thought must be the harder: the heart, the keener.
> Courage shall be greater as our strength grows less.

In estimating the achievement of the Anglo-Saxon period it must be remembered how much of the literature of that time has been lost. Before the printed book all literary survival was most hazardous and one can marvel that so much has come down to us, but the picture that emerges must be very incomplete.

Some French critics have tried to ignore all these early centuries and by emphasizing the Latin side of our tradition would begin the story with Chaucer. It is true that with Chaucer one often moves into a European world, and sometimes as in the *Prologue* to the *Wife of Bath's Tale* with an idiom that is modern in an almost startling manner. But the Northern or Germanic element was there much earlier and to ignore it would be to distort the whole picture. It would also leave out a major part of the Latin influence on English.

V

For while part of this early literature is written in early English, or in Anglo-Saxon as it has sometimes been called, much of it is in Latin. The longest and most important tradition in English literature has been Latin, as indeed it has been in that of the whole of Western Europe. The language of the Christian Church was Latin. In 597, when the migration of the Germanic tribes into Britain was still incomplete, Augustine came from Rome to teach Christianity and landed in Kent. It is reported that Augustine soon had ten thousand converts, which would suggest that, though the language of the Church was Latin, the vernacular was the language of evangelizing. It was in the same period that monks came from Ireland with the Christian message and so began the long cultural debt of England to Ireland.

The greatest of these early Christian Latinists in the pre-Norman Conquest period was the Venerable Bede (672-735), the Northumbrian monk who spent most of his life in the monastery at Jarrow, and wrote apart from lives of saints and abbots and many other works, the great *Ecclesiastical History of the English Race.* Educated with a pious simplicity by Irish Christian monks he had made Jarrow a centre of civilization in a most troubled century. 'There is no period in the history of Britain or of the English Church in which Bede is antiquated,' W. P. Ker writes, 'in every generation he speaks familiarly. The seventeenth century is less intelligible to the eighteenth, the eighteenth century more in opposition to the nineteenth than Bede to any one of them: his good sense is everywhere at home.'[1] Latin was the language of

[1] *The Dark Ages,* 1904.

Christendom until the Reformation. It remained the language of reading and contemplation in later centuries of many English ecclesiastics, including those of the Protestant faith.

The influence of English and the importance of Latin appear very early in the history of England in the work of King Alfred (848-899), the most remarkable of all English kings. He had to face invasion from the Danes, the ruining of towns, villages and churches by pillaging. He had to fight a difficult, delaying action against a ruthless enemy, but, though only a young man, and much harried by danger and the cares of strategy and administration, he encouraged learning in his country's desperate hour. 'No other king of the Dark Ages ever set himself like Alfred, to explore whatever in the literature of Christian antiquity might explain the problems of fate and free will, the divine purpose in the ordering of the world, and the ways by which a man comes to knowledge.'[1] Alfred was helped in his translations from the Latin by learned associates, but the final English renderings are usually his own. He had to build English into a prose instrument. His motives were practical. He describes in the preface to his first translation, the *Cura Pastoralis* how few of the priests know the meaning of the Latin they recite. Most of them cannot translate the simplest passage from Latin into English. Alfred wished to revive scholarship amid the priests, to lead them back from his English translation to Latin. Alfred was not thinking that English would take the place of Latin. Indeed, his great admiration was reserved for the Latin scholarship of the age of Bede. His works were to be the basis from which men could be led back to Latin and in the generation after his death this happened. So Alfred's triumph in the vernacular remains, unfortunately, an isolated incident. Among the works he inspired was the *Anglo-Saxon Chronicle*, a contemporary history

[1]*Anglo-Saxon England* by F. M. Stenton, 1947 p. 267.

of England, with vivid and authentic descriptions of the struggles against the Danes.

As great and possibly even greater was the influence of Latin on secular thought and writing. Even in the late sixteenth century Francis Bacon (1561-1626), who was himself a master of English, is anxious to translate his more important works into Latin, for in that way alone does he feel that their permanence will be secure: he is afraid that English will 'play bankrupt' with him. In the early centuries much of the work in Latin seems of an unexciting character. It is contained in books of instruction, philosophy and history. It is employed for humble and practical purposes. Yet the strength of the Latin tradition can be seen in the popularity and in the survival through the centuries of a volume such as Boethius's *Consolation of Philosophy*.

Boethius himself was a Roman, born in Rome between 470 and 475. A consul in 510 he was looked upon with favour by Theodoric the Great. Later he incurred suspicion of plotting and was imprisoned and finally put to death in 525. It was while he was awaiting death that he wrote the *Consolation*. His work circulated in England in the Latin original, as it did in the other countries of Western Europe. But it was also translated into English by King Alfred who died in 899. So continuous was the popularity of Boethius's work that some five hundred years later his volume was translated again by Geoffrey Chaucer who died in 1400. The third translation was begun by Queen Elizabeth who died in 1603. Few other books in English literature can show such concrete evidence of consistent popularity for a period of over seven hundred years.

Indeed the vogue of Boethius lived on even further. He was part of the reading of educated men in the eighteenth century and in the nineteenth century William Morris reprinted Chaucer's edition and wrote in the preface: 'No philosopher was so bone of the bone and flesh of the flesh of the Middle Age writers as Boethius. Take up what writer you will and you find not only the sentiments but the very words of the distinguished Roman'. Further, as W. P. Ker has indicated,[1] 'Boethius has been traced in English literature from *Beowulf* to *Hamlet* and *Lycidas* "the last infirmity of noble mind" is a quotation, and Hamlet is thought to have had in his tablets, somewhere, *Adeo nihil est miserum nisi cum putes*'.[2] Boethius's work was an allegory of philosophy and contemplation. He pictures Philosophy visiting him in prison. His reflections stretched back to the past, to the world of Greece and Rome, and his mind and imagination answered something consistently in the mood of the centuries that were to follow, and not only in England: to quote only a single example, in Italy Dante was to remember him with honour.

Boethius serves to show how strong and continuous was the influence of the Latin author, not only in England but in Western Europe as a whole. But apart from the influence of Latin in the Church and the influence of secular Latin authors both in the original language and in translation, there was also the widely diffused influence of Latin in the education and in the reading of writers in England even to the beginning of the twentieth century. The only grammar that Shakespeare would be taught at school would be a Latin grammar and the first conscious thinking of a boy in the sixteenth or the seventeenth or even in the eighteenth century about the sentence would be the form of the inflected Latin sentence. How strong was this influence upon a mind that had been thoroughly immersed in these classical studies can be seen in the work of Milton, who writes English prose frequently as if he were handling the long inflected sentence of Latin rhetoric. The editors of Samuel Johnson's poems in introducing their edition

[1] *The Dark Ages*, 1904.

[2] 'For there is nothing either good or bad
But thinking makes it so.' II.2.257.

in 1941 wrote: 'Latin was so much a living language to Johnson, so much a natural medium for expression in certain moods, that to treat his poems in that language as a mere exercise in ingenuity is to mistake their purpose and ignore their intimacy'.[1] Such could be the interests and loyalties of a great master of the English language in the middle of the eighteenth century.

So varied and extensive is this influence of Latin that it is difficult to make any brief assessment of how English literature and the English mind have been affected by this tradition. The benefits are obvious. It was through Latin that England was able to become part of the Christendom of Western Europe and also through the free use of Latin both orally and in writing was able to join in that community of scholarship which existed in Western Europe up to the Reformation. It would have been a wonderful thing for Europe if the tradition of the use of Latin as a living language for communication between scholars in Europe could have continued to the present day. It is true that much was gained in the sixteenth century in England by the increased development of the English language itself and of its brilliant use by the master minds of that time. But if this could have been attained without the loss of the second language for scholarship and generally for international communication the pattern of Europe would have been less divided in the centuries that were to follow.

The more complex and not wholly beneficial influences of Latin on the mind of England from the sixteenth century onwards have not always been fully perceived. It is significant, for instance, that there is no study of the general use of Latin in England. This would seem one of the obvious major tasks of scholarship, but it has never been attempted. This arises because Latin scholars after the revival of learning were interested

[1] *The Poems of Samuel Johnson*, edited by David Nichol Smith, and E. L. McAdam, 1941.

in certain classical authors than in the whole tradition of Latin as a living language within the English cultural and educational system. This arbitrary restriction hardened itself into a discipline of classical instruction which concentrated upon an artificially selected group of writers, particularly Cicero in prose and Virgil, Horace and Ovid in verse. It can be claimed that from an educational point of view much was gained, for these studies led to a lucidity of thought and presented young minds with the pattern of a precise grammatical structure which their own language did not possess. On the other hand, it had certain adverse effects in that it limited the number of Latin authors that were to be studied and insisted that all who were to claim attention must belong to a classical period. Under such a system Erasmus could not be presented as a Latin author. Further, this emphasis upon Latin literature diminished the importance that certain educated sections in England were from the sixteenth to the nineteenth century to attach to their own language. It brought into the education of certain social classes in England a language which seemed to be the prerogative of their own status and in that way helped to divide the talents of England on a class basis. There was no Professorship of English Literature in England until University College London established one in the early nineteenth century, and it has been left to that same College in the middle of the twentieth century to found a Chair which includes the study of the contemporary English language. It may have been this artificiality in the study of Latin that left the subject so vulnerable when in the twentieth century modern studies began to make their major claim upon the pattern of instruction. The regression is much to be deplored for generations that are separated altogether from the study of Latin will be removed from what has been the major and most long continued tradition in English thought.

VI

IT may be asked why, if such importance is given to Latin as part of the English tradition, a similar emphasis is not attached to Greek and to Greek studies. The simple truth is that as far as literature is concerned Greek has had a very minor place compared with Latin in the whole content of English thought and of literature. Greek had no place in the Church, nor in Law, nor was the Greek language ever a commonly accepted and utilitarian means of communication among scholars. The fact that Greek literature itself is far more splendid than Latin has sometimes disguised these facts and has led to their misinterpretation. For instance, among the writers who were Shakespeare's contemporaries in the drama, there were only two who had a mastery of the Greek language, Ben Jonson and George Chapman. Yet there is very little that is Greek in Ben Jonson's (1573-1637) own imaginative creation and when he seeks for classical models in the drama it is to the Latin writer Seneca that he, like his less learned contemporaries, turns. George Chapman (1559-1634) it is true translates Homer into English and his renderings are poems in their own right which have captured imaginations in later centuries and were one of the formative influences upon the developing genius of Keats. Yet Chapman's verses with their diffuse and baroque profusion have but little contact with the Greek ideal as it is commonly represented. Alexander Pope, who again, in the eighteenth century, translated Homer in a somewhat un-Greek manner, was influenced in his own original work far more by Horace and by Latin writers.

In the seventeenth century Abraham Cowley did attempt to penetrate the mysteries of the Pindaric Ode and render them into English but the complex and irregular splendours which he produced have once again very little resemblance to the Greek genius. And when in the eighteenth century a learned writer such as Thomas Gray returns once again to these forms one feels that it is the mechanical side alone which has come from Greece while the imagination is fed by stranger and more romantic sources. It is true that in the nineteenth century a number of writers, particularly Shelley and Swinburne, have an intimate knowledge and deep admiration of Greek poetry and use its forms and motifs in their own verse, but the resulting productions are romantic and not classical in their emphasis. Thus, as far as literature is concerned, Greece has had but a limited influence and one which has been much exaggerated. By an odd irony Keats, who knew no Greek, had a deep admiration for the world of antiquity and in *Hyperion* by some imaginative intuition captured something of the mood of a classical world.

This is not to diminish the effect which from the middle of the eighteenth century to the end of the nineteenth Greek literature had on the minds of young English men whose education was patrician. In the public schools the ablest minds were encouraged to read what was best in Greek literature and to exercise their talents on the composition of Greek prose and verse. Much that is best in the English mind in that century and a half cannot be understood unless this influence is given its due place.

VII

DESPITE all the limitations it can, however, be claimed that literature is the art in which the English have most greatly excelled. Within this art of literature they have been much engaged mainly with the study of human nature, of personality and individuals, and in verse over centuries and in many different ways with forms of romanticism that seem remote from the commercial instincts and pursuits with which in other countries they are so often associated.

In the other arts, in music, in painting and in architecture, there are figures in France, Italy and Germany that surpass those who are of English origin and the tradition has been more continuous in these other countries. It might be claimed that where England has been outstanding in these other arts it has again been in the exploration of some aspect of the personal life of men and women. In architecture, whatever may have been the English contribution to ecclesiastical buildings, the most individual achievement has been in the great country houses of England. In variety, in distinction and in some instances in splendour they are unparalleled in any European country. They far surpass any architectural achievement in the public buildings in England of secular origin. It is further of interest that this most meritorious aspect of English architecture, though it has had for centuries a highly idiosyncratic charm and a great beauty and distinction of its own, must be set in a very individual context and one that cannot have universal appeal, nor indeed is it like the greatest things in art exportable.

Similarly in painting, though the English achievement is wider than is often allowed, its most characteristic form has been in portraiture, which once again is associated with the personal and domestic life.

In 1531 the Convocation of Canterbury recognized Henry VIII as Supreme Head of the Church in England and with Protestantism the painter was no longer welcome to exercise his art among the legends of the Church. There was unhappily no public in England, as there was in Italy, for painting based on classical mythology. Henry VIII's arbitrary nationalism did seem to develop in literature an increased strength which was enhanced, particularly in Elizabeth's reign, by the convictions and sense of power of a newly nascent nationalism, but whatever literature might have been gaining indirectly from these political and other movements, the other arts and particularly the visual arts were losing in their separation from European traditions. Henry VIII did much to discourage and even to destroy in England the tradition of ecclesiastical architecture by his secularization of the monasteries and in the visual arts he wasted the magnificent opportunity offered by Holbein's residence from 1532. The only encouragement he gave to Holbein was in the art of portraiture. Holbein was a German humanist, a friend of Erasmus, whose *Praise of Folly* he illustrated. He had been driven from the Continent by the bleak dissensions of the Reformation. His range was much wider than the portraits he executed at the bidding of Henry and his friends. Even in Stuart times the visual arts were not of native development. One of the glories of Charles I's reign was his great collection of pictures and of other works of art, which were so wantonly dispersed under Cromwell's rule. But again most of his treasures were not of native but of continental origin. Again though Charles I had a wide and exact taste his patronage in painting through Sir Anthony Van Dyck of Antwerp went mainly but not exclusively into portraiture.

If the English failed thus in the sixteenth and seventeenth

centuries in the production of outstanding work in the visual arts, they did not lack, particularly in courtly circles, the desire for colour and pageantry. Queen Elizabeth when she went on her frequent visitations to her noblemen, which were so costly to their purse, set herself into scenes of such pleasing decoration that they would have made admirable conversation pictures had the right artist and the right tradition been present. The great tapestries which decorated Tudor mansions were only one of the ways in which this desire for splendour and colours was satisfied and the elaborate costumes of the courtiers and of their ladies were, similarly, a manifestation of the same taste. Francis Bacon cannot discuss even abstract and philosophical matters without importing images from a sensuous enjoyment: 'Truth may perhaps come to the price of a pearl, that showeth best by day, but it will not rise to the price of a diamond or carbuncle, that showeth best in varied lights. A mixture of a lie doth ever add pleasure.' The miniatures of the Elizabethan artist Nicholas Hilliard (1547-1619) the Queen's 'limner and goldsmith' catch some of this passion for decoration as if all the longing for the visual arts of the Elizabethans had been concentrated into their elaborate garments employing all the embellishments of the Italianate tradition.

This longing for colour and pattern and form was ultimately satisfied, not only through tapestries and garments and pageants and masques, but by a concentration upon words both in prose and in verse but supremely in verse. Indeed, it seems at times as if the Elizabethans were compensating for the meagreness of their resources in the pictorial arts by their concentration of interest in language and in all the multiple devices and pleasant intricacies which it could produce. Fortunately at this time there were in England the men of genius, Spenser, Sidney, Shakespeare, and many men of talent to use the language in a supremely effective way.

So it came about that in the Elizabethan age the art of words in England flourished without the sustaining influence of the other arts, or if this is too absolute a statement, with the other arts in subsidiary forms, such as decoration, costume and the tapestries of the great houses. Further this art of words, which is the art of literature, gained, as has been suggested, great encouragement from the court and from the Queen herself. Yet even in Elizabethan times when literature seems to be so much at the centre of national life it failed to command the attention of the nation as a whole. In later times the court has not often been as genial and as helpful as it was under Elizabeth. The general indifference to secular literature as an imaginative art practised in the vernacular can be well illustrated by the famous library which Sir Thomas Bodley (1545-1613) gave to Oxford. The Bodleian Library was opened in 1602 with more than two thousand volumes, but with no 'riffe raffe' such as contemporary plays and pamphlets. The general catalogue published in 1605, which was apparently the second catalogue issued of a European Library, had six thousand items, but of these only thirty-six were of works in English and only three belonged to English literature, Chaucer's works, Lydgate's *Fall of Princes*, and Puttenham's *Art of English Poesy*.

It is strange that a country which has achieved so much in its literature should yet have regarded contemporary literature so often with indifference or, in some periods, even positive hostility. The national and particularly the governmental attitude to printing and to the general circulation of books was hostile from Tudor times to the beginning of the eighteenth century and censorship has acted in such a capricious form in more recent times that one has reluctantly to regard this as a permanent feature of English life. When the Tudors granted a charter to the Stationers' Company in 1557, it was not with any desire of improving the art of printing or of spreading learning and imaginative literature. The aim was to license, to control and to suppress, and generally to regard the printer as a dangerous man who should be watched most closely. It is true that the government was mainly troubled about works that were seditious, but the restrictions had at least an indirect effect on imaginative literature.

It was on 29th June 1566 that Queen Elizabeth signed a decree passed by the Star Chamber requiring every printer to enter into substantial recognizances for his good behaviour. No books were to be printed or imported without the sanction of a Special Commission of Ecclesiastical authorities under a penalty of three months' imprisonment and the forfeiture of all right to carry on business as a master printer or bookseller. All the profitable work went to a dozen royally privileged printers, who had the exclusive right to print bibles and law books. Later in 1586 all printing was restricted to London and the two Universities of Oxford and Cambridge and all books had to be licensed. Fortunately the effectiveness of both Tudor and Stuart tyranny was modified by the incompetence of the administration, but it was at the same time in an atmosphere of suppression in printing that some of the greatest English literature was produced.

These deplorable conditions did nothing to encourage any skill in the art of printing. The great masters of English literature did not have their works printed in beautiful books. 'The art of printing in England had never at any time such a point of excellence as in Paris under the Estiennes, in Antwerp under Plantin, or in Venice under the Aldi. So great was the competition between the printers, and so heavy the restrictions placed upon them, that profit rather than good workmanship was their first consideration; and when to these drawbacks was added the general disorganization of trade consequent upon the outbreak of civil war, it is not surprising that it failed to maintain even that lower standard of excellence.'[1]

So while Shakespeare touched the resources of language in a way unmatched in any period of English literature, his plays were published in wretched editions that are unsightly to read and whose text was so carelessly reproduced that it has ever since puzzled the ingenuity of generations of commentators. It can, of course, be urged that Elizabethan stage conditions made the publication of plays undesirable to the companies that owned them. But even great compilations such as Shakespeare's First Folio of 1623 and the succeeding Folios, and the 1616 Folio of Ben Jonson, have nothing to match the elegance of the continental presses, and the craft behind them has nothing to answer the genius of the authors. Popular, in a limited way, contemporary volumes of poems and plays may have been, but many a gentleman's library existed in complacent ignorance of their existence. Indeed, a catalogue 'of the most vendible books in England' (1657) 'acclaimed two writers now known only to the specialist in seventeen-century literature, Francis Quarles and George Wither'.[2] Their most popular books appeared both in the year 1635 and each of them was a shining example of a particular category of emblem books. Wither was a Puritan and Quarles a Royalist and they both responded to the taste of their time in adapting the moral tenets of Elizabethan writers. A gentleman's library would have the Latin classics, sermons, discourses, history, politics, even possibly travel, but very few contemporary books and of these still fewer that dealt with imaginative literature.

[1] *A Short History of English Printing*, 1476-1900, Henry R. Plomer, 1915.

[2] The quotation is from *Five Hundred Years of Printing*, S. H. Steinberg, 1955.

IX

It must be easy to exaggerate these difficulties for the writer who did not offend the state could continue with his work and its publication unharmed. What was lacking was the atmosphere of positive encouragement. At the same time, despite all these difficulties English writers were helped both by the nature of their language, and by the way that from the seventeenth century onwards for political and other reasons it has spread from one country to another until in the twentieth century it has become a world medium of communication. Of the genius of the language it is difficult to write adequately in a brief compass. English has readily adopted vocabulary from other languages, and on the basis of Old English, Latin, French and Italian forms, as well as others, have been generously assimilated. This wealth of vocabulary may have led sometimes to a lack of absolute precision, or to those logical qualities which some French prose, and even French verse as in Racine have so admirably possessed. But for the imaginative writer the profusion of the vocabulary, the multitudinous cohorts of words have been a stimulus, though, of course, also a temptation. Yet the greatness of English is that this instrument of prose, which can call out for magnificence with an elaboration in the structure of the sentence and a seemingly infinite variety in vocabulary, can also be employed with power in simple sentences and in words which are mainly monosyllabic. It is the nature of the sentence in the uninflected language which can give to poet and prose writer alike this possibility of endless variety, from plain statement that could be vigorous and forceful, thought unadorned, to complex sentences that sustained their clarity not with the precise sign-posts of an inflected language but by a pattern more individually controlled and often dependent on a rhythmical structure. Not at once did English writers realize the power of the instrument they possessed. The pattern of the Latin sentence was, undoubtedly, a spur to ambition, and this was good. It was from the Latin sentence that King Alfred in the ninth century first learned to build up the elaborate English sentence. But there were dangers and often in the sixteenth and seventeenth centuries it left the writer entangled in his unmastered complexities. Nowhere are the positive advantages of the Latin influence accompanied by its subtle temptations more apparent than in its varying intrusion into English prose style.

As has already been suggested, Milton himself could lose himself in trying to convert too absolutely the pattern of the Latin sentence into English. But at the same time he and some of his contemporaries, at their best, employed all the gothic intricacies of English vocabulary and rhythm in a splendid way which would not have been possible to them without their Latin studies. The following quotation from Milton's *Areopagitica* has two sentences: in the first, Milton is struggling with the pattern of the Latin sentence, and on the most optimistic assessment only just keeping his head above water as far as clarity or even grammar is concerned: in the second sentence, while still elaborate, he comes to a grand and triumphant expression which would have been impossible for him without his Latin studies:

'For as in a body, when the blood is fresh, the spirits pure and vigorous, not only to vital, but to rational faculties, and those in the acutest, and the pertest operations of wit and subtlety, it argues in what good plight and constitution the body is, sc when the cheerfulness of the people is so sprightly up, as that it has, not only wherewith to guard well its own freedom or safety, but to spare, and to bestow upon the solidest and sublimest points of controversy, and new invention, it betokens us not degenerated nor dropping to a fatal decay, but casting off the old and wrinkled skin of corruption to outlive these pangs and wax young again, entering the glorious ways of Truth and prosperous virtue destined to become great and honourable in these later ages.'

Such is the struggling style which from time to time can be transformed in passages such as:

'Methinks I see in my mind a noble and puissant Nation rousing herself like a strong man after sleep, and shaking her invincible locks: Methinks I see her as an Eagle muing her mighty youth and kindling her undazzled eyes at the full midday beam: purging and unscaling her long abused sight at the fountain itself of heavenly radiance; while the whole noise of timorous and flocking birds, with those also that love the twilight, flutter about, amazed at what she means, and in their envious gabble would prognosticate a year of sects and schisms.'[1]

The excitement in Milton's prose depends on the continual anxiety as to whether he is going to be successful or to be overwhelmed by some sentence that goes mounting on with clause after clause, and phrase after phrase to the borders of unintelligibility.

Among his contemporaries, particularly in Sir Thomas Browne, the grandeurs of this prose were employed more rhythmically and securely because the mind behind them was less powerful and so less overwhelmed by the power of the material he had to convey. He also possessed a greater sense of rhythm in prose than did Milton, as he was able, as was Macaulay much later and in a very different way, to relieve the

[1] *Areopagitica.*

pressure of magnificence with simple statements. He could write with a biblical simplicity, as in the passage on God: 'Wisdom is his most beauteous Attribute; no man can attain unto it, yet Solomon pleased God when he desired it.' From this he can move to his elaborate sentences as in the contemplation of Death. He says that he is not afraid of death, and then adds:

'Not that I am insensible of the dread and horror thereof; or by raking into the bowels of the deceased, continual sight of Anatomies, Skeletons or Cadaverous reliques, like Vespilloes,[1] or Grave-makers, I am become stupid, or have forgot the apprehension of Mortality; but that, marshalling all the horrors, and contemplating the extremities thereof, I find not anything therein able to daunt the courage of a man, much less a well-resolved Christian; and therefore am not angry at the error of our first Parents, or unwilling to bear a part of this common fate, like the best of them to die, that is, to cease to breathe, to take a farewell of the elements, to be a kind of nothing for a moment, to be within one instant of a spirit.'[2]

[1]Those in charge of burials.
[2]*Religio Medici.*

X

FROM the seventeenth century onwards certain English writers have continued to develop the elaborate possibilities of English prose and for them even in the eighteenth century the pattern of the Latin sentence continued to serve as a model. Samuel Johnson, particularly in his essays in *The Rambler*, uses the balance and amplitude of the Latin sentence and when he is hurried or wearied their employment becomes more absolute. It was almost as if the shape of the Latin sentence was more natural to him than the idiom of his own language.

Johnson at the same time realized that the genius of the English language was capable of supreme simplicity without any diminution of force and, although this was not the manner which he himself practised, he was capable of admiring it in others. In his *Life of Dryden* he pays tribute to Dryden's prose in such a way that he would seem to criticize his own style in admiring Dryden's easy manner. He writes that none of Dryden's *Prefaces* 'were ever thought tedious':

'They have not the formality of a settled style, in which the first half of the sentence betrays the other. The clauses are never balanced, nor the periods modelled: every word seems to drop by chance, though it falls into its proper place. Nothing is cold or languid the whole is airy, animated, and vigorous; what is little, is gay; what is great, is splendid. . . . Though all is easy, nothing is feeble; though all seems careless, there is nothing harsh; and though, since his earlier works more than a century has passed, they have nothing yet uncouth or obsolete.'

Though Dryden's style was simpler than that of Samuel

Johnson and did not attempt the splendours of Milton or Browne, he yet had many vestiges of antique elaboration. Among Dryden's own contemporaries there had developed a prose which was far more simple than his own and which consciously aimed at clarity rather than elegance. When the Fellows of the Royal Society began to meet from 1660 onwards they found that for the record of their observation and for their proceedings they needed not a language that was ever self-conscious in its elegance but a plain and a practical style. Their first historian, Thomas Sprat (1635-1713) states that it was such an unstarched and unpretentious diction that the Fellows required. Apart altogether from the Royal Society there must have been some elements in the temper of the age that encouraged these virtues of simplicity, for we find a contemporary preacher Robert South (1634-1716) not only exalting plain diction but practising it in his sermons. The same approach to prose is found in the presiding philosophical genius of the age, John Locke (1632-1704) whose philosophy is based much upon the right of each individual thinker to pursue the findings of his own experience, which in return necessitates that this experience should be recorded accurately but without rhetorical embellishment.

As a reinforcement to these considerations the simpler forms of prose were coming into use because prose was being employed for a far wider variety of purposes. It is fortunate that in this period there did develop some men of outstanding genius whose talent gave to these simpler forms of prose qualities of power and effectiveness. Daniel Defoe (1660-1731) is very widely known as the author of *Robinson Crusoe* (1719) but it is doubtful whether in England the extensive range and accomplishment of his work have ever been fully appreciated. He was an imaginative writer, a journalist and in no mean way a thinker.

Defoe, among his other accomplishments, was an excellent

journalist, and with *The Review* established the form, so popular in the eighteenth century, of the periodical essay. He was followed by Sir Richard Steele (1672-1729) and Joseph Addison (1672-1719) in *The Tatler* and *The Spectator*. They were both elegant writers but in their essays addressed themselves specifically to a middle class audience. Nothing was to be made too difficult and style should have transparency even if from time to time, especially with Addison, the temptation to indulge in rhetoric, so near to the heart of a classical scholar, should intervene.

Defoe's contemporary Jonathan Swift (1667-1745) also used direct and simple prose but with far more vigour and brilliance. He showed that prose can be made ultimately dependent upon the mind and the quality of thought rather than upon decorative devices or upon flourishes of rhetoric. Swift had given much attention to the problem of language and its use and among his critical writings is *A Proposal for Correcting, Improving, and Ascertaining the English Tongue.* If these suggestions had been followed England might have had an Academy for the conservation of its language similar to that which is in France.

In much of his writing there is an entirely deceptive simplicity as in the opening of *Gulliver's Travels*:

'My father had a small estate in Nottinghamshire; I was the third of five sons. He sent me to Emmanuel College in Cambridge, at fourteen years old, where I resided three years, and applied myself close to my studies; but the charge of maintaining me (although I had a very scanty allowance) being too great for a narrow fortune, I was bound apprentice to Mr James Bates, an eminent surgeon in London, with whom I continued for four years; and my father now and then sending me small sums of money, I laid them out in learning navigation and other parts of the mathematics, useful to those who intend to travel, as I always believed it would be some time or other my fortune to do.'

This sentence is as long as any one of Milton's most elaborate periods, but it is made up of short phrases, one following upon the other with no balance or superstructure in the period. The reader is carried on by the vigour of the thought and the interest of the matter and in this way the simple style has its own brilliant success. The prose Swift used here for narration could be converted into a prose of power as in *The Drapier's Letters* (1724) where he attacked political corruption and defended the rights of the Irish people. His private writings as in *Journal to Stella* show how sensitive his ear was to the natural rhythm of English speech. He did not impose an artificial design upon the language but rather caught out of conversation and the idioms of English all that was most easy and forceful.

With Swift modern English had developed and his influence was considerable. In the twentieth century W. B. Yeats, when he moved from his early decorative verse to the brilliant and audacious bareness of his later poems, turned once again to study Swift as a guide to 'proper words in proper places'. Somerset Maugham, who in his novels had gained much by the economy of his writing, has confessed that Swift was one of his models.

XI

FROM the eighteenth century onwards English has thus within its own genius been able to develop with many variations from the simple to the elaborate in prose style. The classical manner, as with Milton or with Johnson, has become less frequent. Edward Gibbon (1737-94) did affect the grand style with much success both in his Autobiography and in his History of the *Decline and Fall of the Roman Empire*. But he is far less restricted and rigid than either Milton or Johnson in the patterns within which he moves. He can use the balanced period with complete control, but he can vary it with lightness and brevity or at least with clear sub-division for the ease of his readers. Further like John Lyly with his euphuism in the Elizabethan age he can employ alliteration to create the emphasis that he desires. He calls all these instruments to his service in the magnificent sentence with which he closes the *History*: 'It was among the ruins of the Capitol that I first conceived the idea of a work which has amused and exercised near twenty years of my life and which however inadequate to my own wishes I finally deliver to the curiosity and candour of the Public.'

In the next century Macaulay (1800-59), though again he owes much to the classical manner in his Essays and in his *History of England*, exercises great independence in his manner. He will often take the long period of classical style and break it up into short sentences for the convenience and for the ease of his reader. Few English writers have been more widely read and this in part is a tribute to the vigour and clarity which he was able to impart to all he wrote.

In the nineteenth century and again in the twentieth century there have been great variations of individual style. For instance, a writer such as Charles Lamb (1775-1834) in his *Essays of Elia* (1823) and *Last Essays* (1833) in mock-seriousness revives the grand manner of Sir Thomas Browne and of the majesty of seventeenth-century prose. But this is known by all to be an artifice even if a popular one. Again a writer such as Thomas Carlyle, failing to draw attention to his thought by writing in plain and direct English of which he was a master, developed an odd and idiosyncratic manner of his own, which acted as a sort of neon-lit advertisement to call attention to what he had to say.

In a short survey of the outstanding traditions of English literature it would be impossible to deal with the detailed history of English prose, but the essentials of the picture have already been presented. There is a range and flexibility in the language which will permit of elaborate and highly individual writing, but there is also a sustaining genius in English which yields a vigorous expression within the most simple vocabulary and in short sentences which are devoid of all subordinate clauses.

That this continues in the twentieth century is possibly best illustrated by the fact that C. K. Ogden and James Joyce were contemporaries. Ogden by his invention of Basic English showed how a vocabulary of eight hundred and fifty words could express all ordinary statements in the English language which were necessary for practical purposes. At the same time James Joyce (1882-1941) in *Ulysses* was elaborating English into a complexity which it had not previously endured. Joyce had shown in *The Dubliners* that he could master a style as simple as that of Swift. He worked away from this direct use of speech to invent a language which might serve him as colour and design serves an Impressionist painter. His achievement has been assessed very highly. This at least can be said that in *Finnegans Wake*, his last work, he has led speech to the point of complete disintegration. Prose may develop in many ways, but it cannot go further in the particular direction which Joyce developed.

XII

THE English language has been used in the functioning of parliament and government in a way that is a little outside the range of literature, though it can be urged that what literary historians consider as literature has always been too narrowly conceived. For example, a country, which from the sixteenth century onwards has looked to Parliament as a chamber of debate, has inevitably accumulated much effective oratory on a background of verbal dreariness. In the twentieth century Hansard, which is the report of Parliamentary debates in both the House of Commons and the House of Lords, has every day as many words in the record as would be required by a medium sized novel. Most of this parliamentary verbiage is unreadable, but the exceptions are outstanding. The early records of parliamentary speaking are very incomplete. Fortunately, we do know that in the time of Elizabeth I none of her advisers could match the Queen herself in verbal effectiveness. The greatest of her speeches was delivered not to the House of Commons but in reviewing her army at Tilbury, when although the navy had defeated the Armada it was felt that a danger from Spain still remained. Cynical critics who are familiar with the modern practice of speech-writers may speculate that the Queen was only delivering words which had been prepared for her, but we are assured that this is not so.[1] She used the combined magic of simplicity and rhetoric to encourage her subjects:

'Let tyrants fear. I have always so behaved myself that, under God, I have placed my chiefest strength and safeguard in the

[1] *Elizabeth I and the Unity of England*, J. Hurstfield, 1960.

loyal hearts and good will of my subjects. And therefore I am come amongst you, as you see at this time, not for my recreation and disport, but being resolved in the midst and heat of the battle to live or die amongst you all; to lay down for my God, and for my kingdom and for my people, my honour and my blood even to the dust. I know I have the body of a weak and feeble woman, but I have the heart and stomach of a king, and a king of England too! And think foul scorn that Parma or Spain, or any prince of Europe, should dare to invade the borders of my realm.'

It would be false to suggest that the Queen's subjects often matched her in eloquence. No parliamentary speaker had a greater influence than Edmund Burke (1729-97), yet his most important utterances were in fact carefully prepared pamphlets. Such were the three pieces in which he pleaded for a just and generous settlement with the American colonies in *On American Taxation* (1774), *On Conciliation with the Colonies* (1775) and the *Letter to the Sheriffs of Bristol* (1777). Such again was his attack on the French Revolution in *Reflections on the French Revolution* (1790). Of the *Reflections* John Morley wrote: 'The *Reflections* was no superb improvisation. Its composition recalls Palma Giovine's account of the mighty Titian's way of working; how the master made his preparation with resolute strokes of a heavily-laden brush and then turned his picture to the wall, and by-and-by resumed again, and then again and again, redressing, adjusting, modelling the light with a rub of his finger, or dabbing a spot of dark colour into some corner with a touch of his thumb, and finally working all his smirches, contrasts, abruptnesses, into the glorious harmony that we know.'[1] Burke could indulge in a similar self-criticism on the printed page, but with the spoken voice, and particularly in the House of Commons spontaneity was necessary and

[1]*Burke* by John Morley, 1882.

under such conditions Burke was very much less effective: as Morley says 'In vain did Burke's genius put forth its superb plumage, glittering all over with the hundred eyes of fancy—the gait of the bird was heavy and awkward, and its voice seemed rather to scare than attract.'[1] Burke's gestures were clumsy; he had sonorous but harsh tones; he never lost a strong Irish accent, and his utterance was often hurried and eager. Yet with all these defects he remained the most influential of all English political orators.

In the nineteenth century democracy developed its leisurely oratorical debates. They all seemed very urgent and important at the time and to the speakers themselves. The issue sometimes, in retrospect, seems less important than the verbal virtuosity with which it was handled. Gladstone and Disraeli carried on this stately combat from one decade to another.

The twentieth century was to develop a new audience and new methods. The new audience was to be found in the ever enlarged electorate most of whom could not be usefully addressed in rounded periods and to whom quotations from Horace were meaningless.

[1]*Burke* by John Morley, 1882.

XIII

As has been suggested, the popularity and influence of English literature could not have been such as they are had not the English language spread to so many parts of the world. Throughout North America standards of taste until the middle of the nineteenth century derived largely from England and Western Europe and even after that period English writers continued to hold a position of major importance. It was Edgar Allen Poe (1809-49) who first established in the United States a reputation that would match that of any of his European contemporaries. It is interesting to remember that Poe, who founded an independent literature in the United States, was also the author of that well remembered phrase 'The Glory that was Greece—And the Grandeur that was Rome'. He realized that the origins of Western civilization were in Europe however much he wished to break away from the domination of his English contemporaries. Since Poe's day there has developed an increasing amount of American talent and achievement, so that at the present time most of our popular traditions in literature are dominated by the United States, while in more serious regions of endeavour America has achieved not only a complete national individuality but a vigour and genius which are wholly admirable and to which many English writers have become heavily indebted.

When one moves from the creation of literature to its criticism and to academic studies it can be alleged that in the twentieth century much of the most penetrating work on the classical English writers has been achieved in the United States. Writers such as Horace Walpole, James Boswell, George Eliot and Thackeray, to mention only a few names, have been studied in the United States with an unmatched thoroughness. Such investigations have been based on the numerous manuscript collections which have crossed the Atlantic to be lodged in American libraries. All this free trade in scholarship is admirable and however political changes may affect the future of the English language and its literature there will remain between America and England a common inheritance.

In another way English has become the instrument of development in what were once the British Colonial Territories. Even now that these areas are independent they still employ the English language and their educated minorities still study English literature. It can be confidently affirmed that the best product that the English ever took from their own country overseas was the language and the literature that was written in it. The political oratory of writers such as Burke and Macaulay had a profound influence on the development of Indian thought and of Indian movements towards political liberty. At the same time writers such as Shakespeare and Wordsworth formed part of the educational background of cultivated Indians and helped to serve as some link between the culture of the East and of the West. While Hindi has been proclaimed the official language of India it is to be hoped that English will still continue to be practised as an international medium of communication. English as a language and as a literature has penetrated very deeply into the Indian mind. If that tradition were lost much that is valuable to the human spirit as a whole would perish. In a very different way English has had a profound influence in African territories. The period of contact has been shorter and the background is entirely different, but the need of contact in the future is no less important.

Thus English literature, though it has always had a strongly domestic and at times insular aspect, has become more an international influence than any of the other arts produced in

England. It is the language itself that has made this possible and the language has, from a world point of view, had an influence greater than that of the literature itself. If there is to be a world language medium then that language must be English. History and contemporary usage make that essential.

At the same time the English themselves have never treasured their language as their greatest national asset. Despite Jonathan Swift's advice they have developed no academy for its preservation. They have failed to produce a standard and classless pronunciation. It was left to an Irishman, George Bernard Shaw in the Preface to *Pygmalion* to say that phoneticians 'are among the most important people in England at present'. In the play itself Shaw gave to Professor Higgins, in addressing the cockney flower-girl the glorious speech which defines what English should be: 'remember that you are a human being with a soul and the divine gift of articulate speech: that your native language is the language of Shakespeare and Milton and the Bible; and don't sit there crooning like a bilious pigeon.'

It may be that in the future the English language will have from a world point of view an importance far beyond the literature that has been produced in it in the United Kingdom. It may be that it will change its form in becoming such a world instrument and that it will detach itself from peculiarities of region and class in its use within the United Kingdom itself. Swift pleaded for an Academy of English in England, but what is now needed is an Academy for English as an international language.

XIV

It has been mainly through prose rather than through verse that English literature has become known to readers overseas in European countries, always with the exception of Shakespeare. In imaginative literature the novel has had the greatest influence, and in non-imaginative work, the writings of political orators and scientists. English poetry has not travelled so well and, indeed, to many people overseas the names best known among English poets are those of Lord Byron and Oscar Wilde. One cannot escape the suspicion that the legends of their lives may have proved more attractive than their poetry. They were both rebels in their lives and they both defied the code which traditionally governed English social life and the conventions of private sexual behaviour. Byron had the additional recommendation that he was a Lord and that he ended as a romantic hero identified with the cause of liberty in Greece. Wilde had a career which adapted itself without any modification into legend. Yet by no standard can Wilde be considered a great writer. Much of his verse he plagiarized in a servile way from French and English poets. At his best in such a poem as *The Ballad of Reading Gaol*, he was able to write poignantly on a human theme in a vocabulary which those with only a small command of the language could understand. Byron, on the other hand, especially in *Don Juan* was a great poet, a satirist in verse with a power of manipulating in poetry conversational rhythms and the words of ordinary speech. Even at his lower levels he was a magnificent poetical rhetorician. He has often been admired both in Britain and abroad for his weakest pieces, and to the British ear much of his work is either slack or overemphasized. It may well be that foreigners value the more shallow aspects of his work, romantic narratives such as *The Giaour* because they are so easily intelligible in the same way that the British admire the work of Heine. It is surprising that T. S. Eliot's poetry, despite its difficulties, has had such a considerable vogue outside England.

Apart from the vogue of Byron and Wilde, it is just to claim that English poetry has not travelled abroad as its merits would deserve. It must, of course, be recognized that English verse has had numerous and notable critics in Europe, America and Asia, who have been deeply appreciative, but they have not been able to persuade large and general audiences that English poetry has the originality and imaginative strength which English readers believe it to possess. Yet anyone who would understand England must seek part of that interpretation in its poetry and it is necessary to speculate why foreign readers find this sense of remoteness in English verse.

In the first place the vocabulary of English poetry is not simple. It is true that English possesses no formally distinct poetic vocabulary, although it did so in pre-Conquest verse, but, though for the main part the individual words are the same as those of prose, they are used with different meanings and, where the verse is at its best, in a manner which is vitally metaphorical. Even Wordsworth, who promised to write in the language of ordinary men, came to discover the necessity of using a vocabulary which was highly individualized. He had promised in his preface to *Lyrical Ballads* (1800) that his poems should be chosen from 'incidents and situations from common life' and that these he would relate and describe 'as far as possible in a selection of language really used by men'. By 1806 in contemplating the European situation and his own unrest in 'The World is too much with us' he had recalled a noble Miltonic image to express his thoughts:

Great God! I'd rather be
A Pagan suckled in a creed outworn;
So might I, standing on this pleasant lea,
Have glimpses that would make me less forlorn;
Have sight of Proteus rising from the sea;
Or hear old Triton blow his wreathed horn.

Here he allows all the cohorts of elaborate words to develop his meaning whatever had been his original undertakings to the reader.

Shakespeare is the greatest manipulator of the English tongue in poetry and his popularity abroad would seem to contradict the generalization that is being made. It can, however, be truly said that Shakespeare, as all poets, loses much of his original force in translation, and the number of foreigners who have understood his language in all its innumerable associations is far less than those who have enjoyed the plays. He succeeds because he is so good a dramatist that he remains alive even when the poetic element in his work has been distorted, or even destroyed. Further, his verse has often a meaning so well grounded in human experience that it retains interest even when translation has destroyed much of the original beauty of expression. Thus to quote a single example, Hamlet, at the end of the tragedy, says to Horatio, 'Absent thee from felicity awhile', a phrase which to English minds is of illimitable suggestion. Translate the construction and let Hamlet merely say, 'In memory of this tragedy refrain for a little while from pleasure and happiness', and he is still speaking good sense though he has ceased to speak poetry. Or it may be that Hamlet in that final moment, his stress tragically resolved was referring to death itself as 'felicity'. Should this be the meaning the problem of translation still remains equally difficult.

The supreme power of Shakespeare lies in his command of

imagery to whose functioning he would seem to bring all the experience of his time and all the learning which he found available. This is the secret of Shakespeare which cannot be appreciated unless one is prepared to live with the English language until its most intimate suggestions become intelligible.

In this poetic language English poets have shown that England can produce richly imaginative minds. If their fiction, as will be shown later, illustrates the variety of their life and their social outlook and their sense of compassion, their poetry reveals an inner life, very frequently romantic, sometimes mystical, and ever aware of the poignancy of human existence.

All this depends upon the power of the language for simile and metaphor, indeed, for every type of imaginative comparison. Spenser possessed the gift in common with Milton and, in a very different way, Donne and the metaphysical poets had it powerfully in command. Wordsworth, Coleridge, Shelley and Keats each brought fresh meaning into their poetry by thus exploring further the imaginative possibilities of language. Keats had this control of imagery in a way that is often reminiscent of Shakespeare, and his letters show how he understood that in metaphor, and in all that was associated with metaphor, lay the heart of poetry.

This brief record is not an appropriate place to examine the whole complex problem of metaphor and imagery, for that problem is the most profound and metaphysical that arises in the interpretation of poetry. At its highest, imagery, by drawing together widely separated objects and experiences into a brief and unlaboured expression, asserts the unity of human life. The poet, though often not consciously, is affirming that behind all the conflict of contrasting appearances there is a single life of the spirit. Metaphor is the applied metaphysics of poetry. Imagery in its purest form is mysticism made manifest from sources that depend on ordinary experience. It may well be that it is typical of the British genius that it has discovered this way of making empiricism transcendental. The amorphous and disparate entities of ordinary experience are gathered together into the luminous unity of imagery expressed in poetic language. It would, of course, be unjust to suggest that all English poetry is of this nature, or that the same effects have not been attained in other European languages. Yet, any objective comparison would result in the conclusion that the English language yields itself superlatively to imagery and that English poets have profited by this quality.

It has already been suggested that only a small minority in any country will be the readers of poetry and this is true in England. At the same time it can be urged that in England poetry has been produced continuously for over a thousand years, that, though the audiences have varied in size, they have been continuous, and that the poet, through his medium, has been able to give an interpretation of life. It is clear that some of Britain's most popular poets, such as Scott and Byron, have had little command of this vitally metaphorical use of language. Of all the English non-dramatic poets, probably Pope had the widest audience and Pope used imagery only in a manner that was immediately intelligible to the intellect. This he did with a great brilliance and he succeeded as a critic of the social man. He was achieving in a finely conceived poetic manner the study of man which the novelists in a very different way had achieved in fiction. Byron had ultimately the same purpose in the best of his satire, but his range of human experience was more varied and more entertaining, though Pope reached certain observations of a profundity which Byron could not have attained. What they achieved has been achieved by poets of many other nations. On the other hand, the exploitation of figurative language seems to me the supremely English contribution for which the language itself, flexible, rich in vocabulary, ample in synonyms, suggestive but inexact in reference, offers an unparalleled instrument.

XV

In thus exalting the metaphorical language of English poetry as its supreme achievement and its range in imagery which varies between fancy and imagination, it must at the same time be recalled that some of the supreme effects in English poetry have been obtained by direct statement, and it is again part of the genius of the language that, while it permits of the wide-ranging resources necessary for imagery, it can gain effects of the highest imagination through simple statement. Shakespeare himself in the periods when he was using figurative language with a most daring and original complexity could return again to dramatic effects of supreme force by the use of statements which are made in an order not differing from the order of prose, which are in no way decorated with synonym or metaphor, and which employ the most simple and ordinary words. An outstanding example is the speech made by King Lear when he sees Cordelia on his recovery from madness:

> Pray, do not mock me:
> I am a very foolish, fond old man,
> Fourscore and upward, not an hour more nor less;
> And, to deal plainly,
> I fear I am not in my perfect mind.

John Donne, whose reputation lay largely in the learned and intellectual complexity of his imagery, could yet attain some of his most moving effects by this same use of the genius of the English language in its most simple form. Thus he describes the calm at sea, following a storm, in a passage which movingly combines a vivid and easily intelligible imagery with plain statements of fact:

> And all our beauty, and our trim decays,
> Like courts removing, or like ended plays.
> The fighting place now seamen's rags supply;
> And all the tackling is a frippery.
> No use of lanthorns;[1] and in one place lay
> Feathers and dust, today and yesterday.

It must be admitted that there have been periods when the decorative language of English verse has become an artificial convention and this was the danger that pursued the romantic poets in these periods. It was in reaction against this that some modern writers, notably T. S. Eliot, sought, once again, the genius of the common word, of even the conversational rhythm of English, for the purposes of verse expression. Thus in his poem 'Gerontion' he uses a language which is as simple as the speech which has been quoted from *King Lear*:

> Here I am, an old man in a dry month,
> Being read to by a boy, waiting for rain.

Apart from this manipulation of language, there are other ways in which English poetry is distinctive from that of the rest of Western Europe. It is not that the poets of Britain have kept themselves consciously apart, for they have been great borrowers, but they have at their best transformed what they found, and employed it for their own ends. The debt has been considerable and continuous. Apart from the deep obligation to classical and Hebraic sources, France and Italy have in almost every century since the twelfth given new themes and suggestions for new forms to English poets. If a balance had to be struck it would be just to maintain that the Latin and the

[1]Lanterns.

Italian influences have been the largest and the most profitable. As has already been suggested, Greek, though widely studied in Britain, has had less influence upon poets than is commonly imagined. What has been borrowed has endured a sea-change on its voyage to Britain. The nature of the modification is difficult to define and generalization is here more than usually dangerous. It can be affirmed that the 'movements' and 'schools' which have developed in the literature of Western Europe are not to be found in such an extreme or absolute form in England. It is as if the spirit of compromise, which finds expression in so many phases of the national life, were present also in the approach to literature. The romantic element, for instance, has been present in English literature in some form or another since the Middle Ages, but it has never been so closely defined as in France, nor has the distinction of classical and romantic been so strictly and logically maintained as in France and Germany.[1]

When Britain found the neo-classicism of the Renaissance, it modified the excessive regimentation of that movement with a strong admixture of native themes and forms. Only two English poets, Wordsworth and Dante Gabriel Rossetti, have set out with a definite programme, and it is revealing that they both ended in writing poetry which is far removed from their original theories. Wordsworth began with the declaration that he would state in poetry the experience of ordinary men in the language of ordinary men, but he found himself as a poet describing his own unique intuitions, and he discovered that the communication of this experience needed a highly individualized language which is often as artificial and as elaborate as that of Milton. Rossetti, early in his career along with the other Pre-Raphaelites, asserted that art, and he included poetry with painting, should have directness, truth of nature, and realism.

[1]I have attempted to develop this theme in *Tradition and Romanticism*, 1940.

His own gloomy and mystical mind led him to Dantesque visions filled with airy and intangible symbols. Nothing could be further from the precepts which he had so confidently pronounced. In English poetry the absolutism of a programme seems to give way to the general tradition and the natural development of the individual. This English adoption of some middle way between extremes and absolutes can be found in the poetry of Spenser and Milton. Spenser in his *Faerie Queene* had as his avowed motive the creation of a poem which should have the form of an epic poem as Spenser had learnt of it in the new romantic narrative of Ariosto and in the neo-classical comments on Aristotle's *Poetics*. Such was his intention, but not such was the poem he produced. The reader of the *Faerie Queene* will not be aware of a single narrative with a united design, but of a vast museum of stories, allegories and descriptions, each with its own life and its own gentle wash of coloured words and lazy, multi-coloured movement, without any strong, directive control and ending suddenly not because the design is complete but because the poet can go no further. The English poet who had set out to bring the Renaissance conception of classical form into England has succeeded in writing a poem which exists almost without form, except for such as is given by the individual stanza. It is part of Spenser's genius that he invented the stanza in which this poem is written. Its nine lines are bound up and completed with an alexandrine so that they become in themselves units which have a separate and sustaining life. As one considers the *Faerie Queene* as an achievement, vast, inchoate, incomplete, but strangely beautiful, it would appear that the native tradition had seized Spenser and demanded from him considerable modifications of the original purpose which he had so carefully planned.

The fate of Milton is different, but yet related. For Milton had early the determination to write in English two epic poems and a tragedy in the classical manner. In *Paradise Lost* and *Paradise Regained* he succeeded in creating two poems that have all the elements which he associated with epic, a closely planned structure in heroic style, and a theme historical and universal in its import. In his tragedy *Samson Agonistes* he made a drama on the Greek model as he understood it. Yet, despite the intellectual determination which Milton brings to the fulfilment of these classical ends, the poetry which emerges cannot be adequately described as classical. It is as if, despite all his purposes, the national genius had possessed him. His vocabulary, as Edmund Burke observed, gains its most original effects by a certain obscurity, an absence of precision, as can be found in such a phrase as 'darkness visible'. Satan, with his assertion of his own personality and his courage, heroic even if evil, is a model for later romantic protagonists, and is so used by Byron. It is a strange and unexpected fate for the central figure of an epic devoted to 'justify the ways of God to man'.

It must not be assumed that this capacity of English literature for coalescing one form with another is wholly a virtue, though in the main it may be so. The great merit has been the continuity of tradition: the penalty has been the difficulty with which the tradition can be changed. Change comes slowly into all aspects of British life. To effect change in Britain is like trying to modify the shape of a piece of marble by rubbing it with one's own naked hands. Literary historians have, at times, suggested that at certain periods one form has had an absolute domination in English poetry, but on closer inspection this is found to be untrue. For instance, Alexander Pope might appear to have wrought the heroic couplet into an exclusive form for English verse composition, and it is true that he had a very great vogue, but, actually, even in the years of his greatest popularity, other forms of poetry were widely recognized. To quote only a single example, James Thomson's *The Seasons* began publication in 1726 and had an immediate popularity, which continued throughout the whole of the rest of the century.

In the twentieth century there has been a revolution in English poetry of unusual strength and of precision of definition. It is not without interest that it was led by one of American origin, T. S. Eliot, who in his earliest days was encouraged by another American poet and critic, Ezra Pound. Probably the verdict of posterity will place Eliot much higher as a poet than as a critic and one must expect a certain over-emphasis, even an acerbity, in the criticism of a creative writer. For it is in this way that he defines his own purposes and discovers the perspective for his own work. Eliot had reacted strongly against the romantic tradition in English poetry and from his own studies of French verse and of the English metaphysical poets, particularly of John Donne, and of some of the Jacobean dramatists, he had discovered a verse form which was devoid of decoration and of rhetoric, but which could be used most effectively in satiric and even in comic contexts. Through his manipulation it further became a most effective form for his own contemplative verse. The importance of Eliot's criticism will ultimately thus lie in the strength which it gave to him personally in his creative work, and for this one may forgive the ill-tempered attacks upon Meredith and Milton and upon the arbitrary and self-conscious interpretation of the tradition in English verse which some of his early prose essays show. Some of these less constructive aspects of his work have been followed by younger poets who have often been critics in verse rather than poets, using new forms to advertise new creeds and to attack what went before, rather than to create a positive tradition of their own.

Eliot himself is a poet whose stature cannot be denied. In his early volume *Prufrock* (1917) his clever, satiric, elliptical verse seems to employ the images and references from previous verse in order to tear down and mutilate the past in his own poems. It is as if he were attacking the inadequacy and complacent approach of his predecessors. He did succeed in *The Waste Land* in giving the clearest image of the spiritual vacuity of Europe between the two world wars. His career as a poet is not yet at an end, and already he seems to show poetically a greater respect for that tradition which he has not always esteemed in his criticism.

There was much justification for an attack on certain elements in the past by twentieth-century poets. For instance, the romantic tradition, as it had appeared in Tennyson, Rossetti and Swinburne, and in so very many minor poets of the nineteenth century, had been overplayed. As sometimes before in English literature, the national tradition for compromise had allowed an outworn and conventional way of writing to continue long after its usefulness was at an end. The directness and persistence of the attack by younger poets might be taken as a token of an increased alertness and directness of a younger generation in England to life as a whole. If so, it would be unwise to discourage it. At the same time, as has already been suggested, if one were to accept all of Eliot's strictures one would be deleting a very considerable amount of English literature which had the approval of centuries behind it. It may ultimately be found that Eliot's major contribution as a poet lies not in the early satiric verse nor even in *The Waste Land*, though that poem will always have a symbolic relationship to his generation, nor even in the verse plays from *Murder in the Cathedral* onwards, popular though these have been and considerable in their effect upon the English theatre, but in the philosophical and contemplative poems of his middle period, entitled *Four Quartets* (1946). These poems are of great originality and distinction. Their introspective analysis is combined with philosophical reflection but is transformed by the verse and by its slow and haunting rhythms into a statement that belongs not to argument but to the living world of the imagination.

The greatest poet, as has already been suggested, that the twentieth century has yet produced is W. B. Yeats, and he contrived to find his way out of his early romantic manner to a clean, severe, unrhetorical poetry without any aggressive attack upon the decorative way of writing which he was abandoning. No poet came ultimately, and particularly in his old age, to a more fresh and comely way of writing, and few poets have looked back more genially upon the past, for Yeats recalls in his verse at different times his great predecessors from Chaucer onwards. As a young man, he had moved in the London of the 'Nineties and had written the romantic lyrics that answered contemporary taste and which still, despite all changes of fashion, retain their validity. A poem such as *The Lake Isle of Innisfree* has been so popular in its time and so often repeated that all has been done to destroy it, and yet, despite all this, it contrives to retain some of the romantic charm which it must have had for its first audiences. Though Yeats as an Irishman had been fully aware of the contemporary scene and, indeed, had ultimately moved as a Senator in his own country, he contrived to retain a personal and even mystical approach towards experience, which, whatever its strength as a philosophy or a faith may have had, permitted him to gain images for his later verse which are of singular beauty. In some poets, the technical performance hardens with old age, but with Yeats in some strange and reassuring way his control over verse strengthened as he grew older. Often a simple but masterly audacity is to be found in his later volumes such as: *The Wild Swans at Coole*, *Michael Robartes and the Dancer*, *The Tower* and *The Winding Stair*.

In the discussion of poetry it is well to remember that verse is not widely read in Britain today; no poet commands the wide audiences of Scott, Byron and Tennyson or even of

John Masefield in his early period. No lyric writer today can appeal to the very varied audience that A. E. Housman commanded in a volume such as *A Shropshire Lad* (1896). The much despised poets of 'the Georgian group', who wrote during the age of George V, had a much wider audience than is possessed today by the poets who have condemned them. It is symptomatic that Rupert Brooke, against whom much of the attack has centred, still continues to be read, and his poems are still bought after a period of nearly half a century after his death while present-day poets are condemned to write to small circles or even to a coterie. An outstanding example of this narrowing audience for poetry can be seen in the reputation and posthumous success of Gerard Manley Hopkins. His biography has been fully explored, his Letters have been published and there have been many critical articles and volumes about his very original verse. Yet, it is surprising how small a number of his poems have been sold during those same years. The large reading public in Britain is a public for fiction and not for poetry and it may be that the audience for fiction is itself declining. No longer does poetry enter into the national life of the Court and of the circle of the ruling elements in the country as it did in the Elizabethan age and even to the early eighteenth century. The space given to poetry in journals and magazines is meagre and the broadcasting services have been unadventurous in making poetry available to their large audiences; while television, which is the dominant form of entertainment and of culture in England at the present time, has found no place for poetry at all. The protection of the poetic tradition has been left in the main to scholars, and within their limits they have approached their task conscientiously. They have produced more accurate editions of the poets of the past than were earlier available, and the sober and honest editorial tasks have been accompanied by valuable interpretation. This academic duty has been carried out also in the United States with what must be described as at least equal conscientiousness as in this country. Yet, the academic preservation of poetry must at its best be an arid activity unless it is related to a living tradition. When Sir Herbert Grierson edited the poems of Donne he was contributing to the active tradition as his work deeply affected the developing imagination of T. S. Eliot and of other poets. But the more routine work upon past poets can have but little relationship to the contemporary scene and to the active penetration of poetry into the contemporary experience. Poetry should live on the lips of the people as well as in the definitive editions of scholars. Industry, commercialism and science have all aided one another in driving underground the life of myth and of the imagination. It would seem that at present civilization is living, as far as the imagination is concerned, on the accrued capital of past generations.

It is dangerous and, possibly, inappropriate at this place to undertake any exercise in prophecy. All one can assert is that much that is most valuable in the spiritual tradition of England is to be found in its poetry. For instance, it is English poetry that expresses the deep affection which the people of Britain have for centuries felt for their own countryside. Though from the time of Elizabeth I the English have been voyagers and travellers and in the eighteenth and nineteenth centuries have settled in various parts of the globe, these activities are represented only in a most marginal way in their verse. The consistent attachment has been for the unaggressive beauty of the English rural scene. Even when the English have been forced to live in towns, as has increasingly happened in modern times, they have remained countrymen at heart. It may be that now in the second half of the twentieth century this sentiment is diminishing, but it remained firm during the period of the Industrial Revolution and even into the early decades of the present century. Already in the fourteenth century the sound of birds and the sight of the green fields appear in the poetry of Chaucer and these things have remained. Shakespeare in *A Midsummer-Night's Dream* idealized that English scene in a way that has entered genuinely and permanently into the national tradition. Thomson and Gray captured into verse all the growing sensibilities which men in the eighteenth century felt in their contacts with nature, and Cowper, Goldsmith and Crabbe continued in various ways the same attachment. With Wordsworth this deep union with nature, as it revealed itself in the rural scene, grew into a faith which had both mystical and moral aspects. This friendly contemplation of nature was possible only in a country which had a temperate climate, where the sun was not hostile and where the landscape never presented itself as a dangerous enemy of man. When at the beginning of the war of 1914-18 a young English poet thought of what he was leaving and what he was fighting for, it was the sights and sounds of the English countryside that came most prominently to his mind. Rupert Brooke has been attacked by many a younger critic, but he was in the great tradition when he thus recalled the memories of rural England. This nature poetry of England cannot be easily exported, for in other climates the gentle friendliness of nature in England cannot be easily comprehended. It must be difficult to understand Wordsworth's poetry of the Lake District when one is in the middle of an Indian summer in the plains. Yet the visitor from overseas who travels in England will soon realize how this long continued affection for nature has arisen among English poets and will realize that if it were to die out there would be a deep spiritual loss in the English tradition. Yet the danger does remain that in modern times, as the great mass of the population crowds into cities, the poet who depends on rural associations may inevitably find himself adrift from the life of his countrymen.

Closely allied to this affection for nature and with a tradition which is as long standing is that element in English verse which for lack of any closer definition may be called English Romanticism. In this must be included the presentation of sentiment which Chaucer already possessed and which continued through Shakespeare to Keats and to Shelley. It was to be rediscovered, moralized and somewhat mutilated in the poetry of Tennyson. This romanticism admitted an idealization of life, an assertion of a faith not fully substantiated by any basis in fact, that life has beauty, glamour, graciousness and an indefinite range of sensibility. It is the belief in courtesy as Chaucer understood the term, and in gentility, and an affirmation that man is more than a machine or a collection of reflex actions. In his perception of the world, in his affections and in his passions, the romantic poet asserts that man is capable of magnificence. The satirist, even indeed the realist, can easily deny this vision and much in the daily incident of life contradicts it. Further, it is a vision which can easily become corrupted and easily run into shallowness. Only by holding to the rare moments when outward circumstance and inward feeling unite in some sensation of exaltation can this faith be maintained.

XVI

THE general features which constitute the unity of English literature are difficult to isolate, and any attempt must obviously be incomplete and open to criticism. In the first place, there has been a constant and enduring interest in the individual man. Very early in English literature this individual voice can be heard, and it is a voice that has never been silenced. The pilgrims whom Chaucer described as they travelled to Canterbury are part of an unending succession. The Wife of Bath spoke the first psychological monologue in English literature, and that study of the individual mind has not ended, not even with the notorious meditations of Marion Bloom in James Joyce's *Ulysses*.

This faith in the individual life is probably the most permanent and secure element in the Englishman's unwritten spiritual creed. It enters into his fiction, his drama, his poetry: it informs much of his history, and accounts for the English passion for biography and autobiography. It is proper that the English should possess so many diarists, memoir-writers and autobiographers, with Samuel Pepys supreme among them. Pepys was a civil servant, a scholar, philanderer, a lover of the arts, and one of the founders of the modern Navy; he was a President of the Royal Society and a collector of ballads, and all that interested him he set down in secret and without shame, from clothes and plays to sermons, from the Fire of London to a casual amorous encounter. He asserted as it were unconsciously, the supreme importance of the private life of the individual, and the human mind itself gained thus an acquisition which it should not easily sacrifice to any ideology whose aim is to reduce life to the colourless uniformity of the mass.

This same interest in the individual has led to the attachment of the English to the art of biography. James Boswell achieved a triumphant realism in his *Life of Johnson* and has thus been able to give his hero a permanent place in the affections of the English people. Yet this interest in the individual has its dangers. Biography, for instance, which can be a great work of art, may descend into the regions of dullness and deceit. Many lives in England have been recorded to construct a portrait of respectability which any discerning eye must know to be untrue. Such a practice of eulogy was prevalent in the nineteenth century when biographers, though they omitted so much in the lives they were recording, seldom contrived to limit their narratives to less than two large volumes.

Though one convention has led to this idealization of the dead, we have also had to endure the reaction which converts biography into satire. Much that was most brilliant in the biography of the twentieth century could be defined as venomous portraiture, where the desire was to make the dead as unheroic as possible. Lytton Strachey, who died in 1932, devoted a talent in prose of a very high order in *Eminent Victorians* (1918) and *Queen Victoria* (1921) to demonstrating that the dead were not as great as either they or their contemporaries believed them to be.

The interest in the individual has led to the great popularity of the novel in England. That increased exploration of the personal life which appears in Pepys and Evelyn and the other seventeenth-century diarists seemed naturally to lead in the same direction, as did many of the periodical essays of Addison and Steele. All this led to the novel coming to its own in the eighteenth century as the vehicle of exploring the personality, motives and above all the sentiments of men and women, who would have been described as 'ordinary' had they not now been presented in depth. Daniel Defoe, whose work has never been sufficiently appreciated in England, led the way.

To many English minds the greatest English exponent of the novel in the eighteenth century was Henry Fielding who in *Tom Jones* (1749) portrayed the frank and honest virtues and failings which the English would claim, particularly the virtues, as their own. *Tom Jones* is a fine, massive, convincing narrative but probably a wider international audience has attached itself to Samuel Richardson. He was a pioneer with *Pamela* in 1740 and ever since that date the novel in one form or another has maintained a circulation and a large audience. Richardson analyzed sentiment, particularly in *Clarissa* (1747-48), in a way that appealed to his age but also added to the general knowledge of human life. The irony which Richardson missed, entered into Laurence Sterne's *Tristram Shandy* (1760-67), one of the most original books of the century, and irony he varied with sentiment and found as a result many readers overseas for his *Sentimental Journey*.

From Richardson's successful venture, when the eighteenth-century printer found himself a novelist almost by accident, the novel has been used for varied purposes from preaching and politics to phantasy and melodrama. With all these diversities the main stream has remained with the life of the individual man and woman, and though Englishmen have gone to the ends of the earth, the main interest of the novelists themselves and of their readers has been with Englishmen in England. It must be admitted that the English novel has never reached that complete vision of life which Tolstoi attained, nor has it penetrated to the metaphysical depths which Dostoevski commanded. Yet the novel in England has amplitude and variety, and in the innumerable works of talent and the many of genius which it contains it represents much of the national character.

The English have not as a nation been attracted to abstract

thought; they have preferred to review life empirically in the terms of actual experience. The greatest mind of the age which produced the Authorized Version was that of Francis Bacon, and it is interesting to speculate why in his own country he has never had the reputation which his genius deserved. It may be that he has suffered because many of his most notable works were in Latin, but enough remains in English to show that the modern world in its philosophical and scientific thought originates more in his work than in that of any other single mind. Further, he was the master of a prose style, coloured, imaginative and compact. In an age when much of our prose was uncertain even when brilliant, he showed a disciplined mind in control. May it not be due to the fact that the English judge greatness by personality rather than by any qualities of pure intellect?

It is therefore appropriate that they should often translate their philosophy into the scenes of life in fiction. George Meredith and Samuel Butler, the author of *Erewhon* which was published in 1872, are two of the most prophetic minds in the nineteenth century, but both set out their ideas, not in philosophical theses, but in novels. Meredith perceived that the ideas of evolution, and of man's biological origin, necessitated a new morality. Man, he affirmed, must realize his organic relation with 'Earth', and must discipline himself to a full and ordered life by a vision of those beginnings. Above all he must not escape to a conceited conception of super-naturalism or to the self-consoling deception of sentimentalism. Samuel Butler, with even greater clarity, perceived that material 'progress' in Western Europe in the nineteenth century was leading to the domination of the machine over man. Like Meredith, he was pleading for a new morality by which man might subdue the machine instead of becoming its slave.

This propagation of thought through the novel has had

certain disadvantages. For in the clothing of fiction, ideas are apt to lose their urgency and their potentiality as a basis for action. The ideas of Meredith and Samuel Butler became part of a liberal movement of ideas, notions acceptable but not practical, instead of encouraging effective action by which our civilization might be led to more desirable ways. The same danger can be found in the adaptation to fiction of much that is most encouraging in English political thought. In the nineteenth century Benjamin Disraeli and Charles Dickens both afford examples of this tendency. Disraeli in *Coningsby* (1844), *Sybil* (1845) and *Tancred* (1847) had advocated a new conception of English nationality to eliminate the divisions of class which made the country two nations instead of a single unity. As a political programme the principles he advocated were admirable, and, had they found adoption in the mid-nineteenth century, England might have made a richer contribution to twentieth-century Europe. Such conceptions, to be effective, needed, however, the powerful advocacy in the political field of a leader convinced of their urgency. In the form of fiction they were masquerading, disguised as notions only on the borderland of reality.

Charles Dickens's contribution to the fiction of ideas is somewhat different, for his novels, by their satire and humanitarianship, profoundly affected his age, and removed from industrial life in England some of its cruelty and its indifference to the welfare of individual men and women. In an age when commercialism was rampant and man was being driven to serve the indifferent Moloch of the machine, he aroused the vision, which is the supreme element in Christianity, of the importance of the individual soul. Fiction has probably never made a greater contribution in effecting some improvement in the conditions of life. At the same time it is clear from Dickens's letters that he saw further than his novels might suggest. He was more of a Radical than he was prepared to admit to his public, and he knew in his own heart that change must come not only in men and women but in the system in which they lived.

I have emphasized this limitation of the novel in English national life, for it is seldom admitted, and it is not without importance. Given a human situation the Englishman sees clearly, and if that human situation can be solved in human terms he will deal with it successfully. If, however, the human situation has to be translated into abstract terms or arouses fundamental considerations, he is apt to become distrustful. As a result, in fiction he has been more occupied in seeking out the defects of his own national system than in attempting any radical basis of reform. The English novel is full of criticism of England, to such an extent that the habit may well be misleading to a foreigner. The English novel from the eighteenth century to the present day is full of a satire by Englishmen on Englishmen. Foreigners have often accused the English of being conceited, arrogant and self-opinionated. A course of reading in English fiction would suggest that this is far from the truth. Peacock, Dickens, Thackeray, Meredith, H. G. Wells, John Galsworthy, Somerset Maugham are only a few of the writers who grew rich by telling their fellow-countrymen how inadequate they were. On the other side, as one who thought well of the English and their mission, Rudyard Kipling stands almost alone.

When analysed the element of satire in the English novel will be found as an attack based not against the nation as a whole but against some particular class. John Galsworthy began his *Forsyte Saga* with the belief that he hated the upper middle class; H. G. Wells has attacked mainly those in official positions; Somerset Maugham, though obviously he takes a mean view of humanity as a whole, concentrates his main attack on the English who live abroad. The conclusion to which one is inevitably led is that the English have failed to produce a novelist who is passionately attached to the national tradition as a whole. The novelist has too often borne the impression of the class in which he was nurtured, looking with suspicious eyes on those above or below him in the social order.

This can be seen in the very different view of life presented by two such modern novelists as Aldous Huxley and D. H. Lawrence. The favoured child of Eton and Balliol seems to have no contact with the son of the Nottingham miner. It can, however, be stated in truth that in the England which is developing in this present age these divisions are breaking down. The worlds into which Huxley and Lawrence were born were as different as the 'two nations' of which Disraeli had written and yet the two men met, exchanged ideas and were friends, and the miner's son was able powerfully to affect the cultured and erudite mind which had developed within another tradition. In this increase of sympathy, this broadening from a class to a national awareness, lies the most promising element in English fiction. It can be seen in the development of Virginia Woolf, who gathered into her later work such a delicate and sensitive picture of English life as a whole. The modern novelist has become adventurous in form and in interpretation. Such an original talent as that of James Joyce cannot probably be imitated, for he had reached the end of his road, but he has shown to those who came after that the older patterns of fiction could be broken to pieces. He had aligned fiction to a metaphysical idea, more closely than ever before in English, and in *Ulysses* he had expended his genius on the fullest interpretation in English literature of the individual man. Living as he did in Dublin and on the Continent, he contributed little to the interpretation of English life in its narrower sense. Yet the way had been shown for the novel to give a full, realistic picture not of one aspect but of the whole of the national life.

Apart from all these considerations of ideas and philosophies, the English novel has had a rich and happy existence. Even the English interest in the individual, in his comic, odd and unaccountable moments, has been maintained. From Fielding and Sterne in the eighteenth century, whenever man has been eccentric, amusing or affecting, the English novelist has pursued him with a lively understanding. Even Sir Walter Scott, who portrayed adventure and romance, gained some of his most secure effects in describing ordinary Scottish people, and in showing that he understood their peculiarities of habit and speech. Dickens discovered his genius in its freest employment when he depicted the comedy of human life, with Mr Pickwick, the Don Quixote of ordinary life, as a supreme example. Even H. G. Wells, who was a chronic reformer, was at his happiest with such a figure as Kipps, the epitome of the ordinary man, and he presents him with comedy but never with cruelty. This unceasing tradition of humour which is at the same time interpretative may account for the absence of any great tragic tradition in English fiction. Laughter breaks in so often that tragedy cannot be maintained. The value of this capacity for discovering comedy in the grimmer situations of life need not be emphasized. On the other hand, the refusal to follow through a tragic situation as tragedy is puzzling. The admixture of comedy in Elizabethan tragedy aroused the condemnation of critics of the neo-classical school, and it was left then for Dryden to explain that the mixture was natural to the national temperament. At the same time Thomas Hardy, who has approached genuine tragedy in such a novel as *Jude the Obscure*, has been little esteemed outside England. He seems often to force his characters to become the gloomy, human symbols of his own pessimism. His popularity may appear to deny the generalizations I have been making, yet it must be remembered that his attraction for English readers lies not solely in his tragic themes but in his wonderful power over detail and anecdote, and his picture of English rural scenes. Often his work has a certain quiet humour, though irony is mingled. Apart from all these considerations, the greater proportion of English fiction has been written with the direct purpose of story-telling, and in the hope of giving amusement to the reader. In English drama, once, in the person of Shakespeare, there appeared a writer who could combine this motive of entertainment with the highest effects of imaginative creation. English fiction has not been so fortunate. In Scott, Great Britain posessed a writer so fecund in the resources of his narrative that at his best he could command a European audience. But the profundities are absent: when the reader turns from the novels to Scott's own *Journal* he realizes that he has been living in a world of romance. The invention in Scott's novels was miraculous, and from the first the legions of imaginative incident were marching through his mind, but the depths of the human heart, the ultimates of joy and sorrow, these were shut out of his romances as if they were enemies to be barred out of a castle where all was dedicated to pleasure.

Scott had among his contemporaries Jane Austen (1775-1817) whom some would rank as among the greatest of English novelists. Her five main novels, *Pride and Prejudice*, *Sense and Sensibility*, *Mansfield Park*, *Emma* and *Persuasion*, have won a distinctive place in the hearts and even in the memory of successive generations of Englishmen. Many can quote large stretches of her narratives. Men bred on the classics who look disdainfully on English literature will yet treasure her work as a thing apart. She lived through the Napoleonic Wars and her brother was a sailor with Nelson but it is the engagements of domestic life that occupy her. She is exquisitely conscious of what her art demands in structure and phrasing. Her dialogue is brilliant, her irony telling but never excessive. Seldom has an artist so completely achieved the task proposed.

Since Jane Austen's day, women have increasingly been the authors of much that is most interesting in English fiction. Among the more recent examples Virginia Woolf had developed a genius for setting modern English figures in relation to their past tradition, and her last work shows how her art was maturing, and how much her death is to be regretted. She was the latest member of a distinguished company in which the three Brontë sisters were the most remarkable. In *Wuthering Heights* Emily Brontë raised the novel to a product of pure imagination by an uniqueness of vision altogether unintelligible in the terms of her experience. Anne had a more ordinary talent, though greater than is often allowed, while Charlotte in *Jane Eyre*, even if she lacks the complete originality of Emily, has written a novel which holds the mind and the senses by the strength of its impact. If the Brontë's possessed more genius than intellect, 'George Eliot' (Mary Ann Evans) had probably the profoundest mind and the widest learning of any woman who has practised fiction in England. Her mind appears ultimately to have weighed down her imagination. In her early work, in *Adam Bede*, she gave the promise of being able to combine vision, integrity and humour, and later in *Middlemarch* she was near to giving to the English novel the expansiveness and realism of Balzac.

I have already protected myself with the plea that this is not a history but a brief account of some of the leading characteristics of English literature, and yet in considering the novel so many names crowd in to be remembered that the temptation of making a catalogue is almost irresistible. Variety extends from John Bunyan, who in the seventeenth century in *Pilgrim's Progress* used his great talents as a natural realist to write a spiritual allegory, to Daniel Defoe, who, a Puritan in origin and remaining so in one corner of his mind, wandered into the paths of adventure and picaresque record in *Robinson Crusoe* and *Roxana*. The English novel has been a portmanteau for many aspects of the national life and thought into which almost anything has been allowed to go. So Arnold Bennett was able to portray the Midlands in *The Old Wives' Tale*, and E. M. Forster, in *A Passage to India*, to give a sensitive corrective to Kipling's picture of the Indian scene.

XVII

It is through drama that England gained the figure who has won universal acceptance for Shakespeare has been by universal consent admitted into the supreme and limited circle of world artists. So much has been written about the plays of William Shakespeare (1564-1616) that any brief notice here may seem valueless, and yet it is impossible to write of English literature without re-defining his contribution. Shakespeare was on the one hand so very English, and yet in other ways he transcended the limitations which have restrained so many of his countrymen. He was above all a man of the theatre, who realized how a play could be composed so that his audiences would be entertained and yet his own genius unrestricted. In a country where the consciousness of class division was strong he discovered how, within a single play, pleasure could be given to the crowd through farce and a strong plot, and to the most discriminating by a subtle analysis of characters or by a transfiguration of language. He appealed to the moral attachments of his countrymen by frequent speeches on moral themes and yet gave to his characters freedom, in their nobility and evil, to traffic as they would wish. He was ever conscious of the divine ordinance to the universe, and yet he never intruded one view of dogma or theological instruction as a preliminary obligation on his audience. He seems to have been able to conceal his own personality in order to create the world which the play in hand demanded. This universality of awareness is coextensive with that which Tolstoi displayed in his novels, but Shakespeare seems less committed than Tolstoi to a moral code. Yet his art maintained a consistent relation to ideas, a vision which varies from one play to another but maintains an underlying consistency. From the first he has observed the conflict in life between reason and passion, and the helplessness of reason when once passion was strongly aroused. Involved in that conflict he saw the conception of loyalty without which life would deteriorate into chaos, and chaos, whether in the individual or in the state, he dreaded. In the comedies he portrayed loyalty affected by passion, and in the tragedies and the historical plays he saw this same loyalty as the victim of intrigue, ambition and the lust for power. He extricated himself from the limitation which any dogmatic adhesion to this conception of loyalty would have imposed upon his art. His characters were to be portrayed with freedom whatever their treacheries might be, as if the dramatist himself were at once the detached spectator and an actual participant in the crisis.

This conception gave his art unity despite its multifarious variety. This vision may deepen and the technical skill increase, but it is the same man who portrays *Henry VI* (Parts I, II, III) and *King Lear*. He began his career probably by collaborating with other dramatists, using the chronicle method of the older history plays, until with Marlowe's example to aid him, he discovered in *Richard II* and *Richard III* how history could be combined with the tragedy of a single outstanding personality. In the *Henry IV* plays he found a method, original in its invention, of balancing one character against another, and so uniting the individual to the larger issues of history. Further, he found through Falstaff how the high-sounding ambition of monarchs and the pretensions of 'honour' could be contrasted with the comic egoist who regarded his own pleasures and comfort as the sole end of life. In this long discipline of the history plays he had discovered all that the conception of loyalty implied for him, and he defined also what may be described, if the term is not interpreted too precisely, as his philosophy of humour. He had, moreover, given in these

English history plays the fullest picture of England which any writer has attained.

He had already practised comedy, beginning with *Love's Labour Lost*, which some regard as his earliest play. In it he had invented a new form of comedy that exploited the wit of words and played with the affections of courtly manners, without making any excessive demands on plot. There is much to suggest that in comedy he experimented freely, as if not fully content with any work he produced. So he passed from the gay animalism of *The Taming of the Shrew* to the elaborate machinery of *The Comedy of Errors*. Such experiment matured in the confident beauty of *A Midsummer-Night's Dream*, in whose perfection he gathered so much of English life from the rustic to the court and beyond to that faery mythology which still remained living in the England of his day.

Later the vision was to deepen, but not before he had added to his comedies the three delightful plays of *Much Ado About Nothing*, *As You Like It* and *Twelfth Night*. All that romantic comedy could yield he imparted to those plays. Reality he excluded, so that sentiment, humour and a fair wash of coloured words might have their freedom to circulate. He knew that the world contained much that lay outside, cruel, ugly and severe, but for a while it was excluded. Already in *The Merchant of Venice*, Shylock stepped with his realism into the make-believe atmosphere to show that the romantic world of Bassanio, judged by any other standards but its own, was shallow. Later in *Troilus and Cressida*, *All's Well* and *Measure for Measure* Shakespeare permitted a harsher vision to enter, while retaining the earlier romantic form of plot which once he had used in a more light-hearted way.

As the vision deepened he moved from comedy to tragedy. In *Julius Caesar* he discovered an interpretation of the Roman world, and in the figure of Brutus he attained a deeper conception than before of the tragic characters. There followed the great tragedies, which have been more universal in their appeal than any other element in his work. Of these *Hamlet* is the earliest and, whatever may be said of its imperfections by imperfect critics, no manifestation of the dramatic genius in modern times has produced a work of such appeal. Around the main action the play gathers a varied and attractive world into which the whole Renaissance atmosphere in its humours, its intrigue, its interest in art, language and superstition, gains ample illustration. At the centre is Hamlet himself, melancholic, introspective, witty, incomprehensible and gracious, that strange, unaccountable Renaissance prince in whom, by some unfathomable miracle, Everyman not only in England but wherever the play is enacted, finds his own image.

There followed *Othello*, more compact and domestic in its theme, but masterly in its power of the stage, and in the contrast of the noble but simple Blackamoor with the subtle and corrupt Italianate mind of Iago. In *Macbeth* he attempted the portrayal of a figure less worthy, and perhaps less attractive than any of the other tragic protagonists, yet in its representation he raised his verse to a greater union of imagination and dramatic effect than ever before. In *Lear* he seized a wider and more primitive theme, lifting his drama in the storm scenes and their aftermath to a vision of life, symbolic almost in its implication, displaying humanity in an intimate union of cruelty and tenderness, while adding a hope of reconciliation and redemption. With *Coriolanus* and *Antony and Cleopatra* he returned to Roman themes. In *Coriolanus* he wrote more severely than in the earlier tragedies, displaying a character proud, noble but defective in conflict with a political world which was defective but not noble. In *Antony and Cleopatra* he called upon all the resources of his art to show passion as it breaks its way through strong and mature natures. It was as if he recalled the adolescent love which he had imagined in *Romeo and Juliet* and was now determined to add the more destructive passage of love in an older man and woman who incorporated in their own persons the destinies of nations. Something brought this tragic period in Shakespeare's art to a close. Many explanations have been given of that change, but none of them is based securely on fact. All that is known is that his career as a dramatist concluded with two plays, *The Tempest* and *A Winter's Tale*, which avoid the ardours of the tragedies. They seem consciously to exclude part of the vision which he had once known. Thus in the quiet beauty of *The Tempest* with its emphasis on forgiveness and reconciliation the evil forces led by Caliban are controlled with an ease which unfortunately is not possible in life itself. Whatever their meaning in relation to his career as a whole, they retain dramatic invention, and *The Tempest* particularly has originality of form, while its theme has been found illimitable in suggestion.

Shakespeare's supreme place in English drama may have served to obscure somewhat the range of that drama as a whole, though dramatic historians have been markedly competent and industrious in presenting the complete picture. The English drama, as far as it is known from extant examples, begins in the Middle Ages, and there have been preserved in England a numerous though not necessarily a representative collection of miracle and morality plays. The miracle plays, based on the themes from the Scriptures, were enacted at certain festivals by members of the trade guilds. The records show that the writers had talent in plenty, and one of them at least, the anonymous author of *Secunda Pastorum*, which shows the shepherds visiting the infant Jesus, had dramatic genius of an unusual order. The place of these religious plays in the history of the English drama has been fully conceded; sometimes, indeed, too much has been made of it. What has not been recognized so adequately is that here in this drama the stage was a genuine element in the social structure. In later ages the theatre had to struggle with the Church and the State, and the theatre is removed from its natural place in the national life. In Elizabethan times the plays were condemned by the Puritan authorities, and the players were in danger of being classed as vagabonds. In the eighteenth century Walpole's government crippled the theatre with a Licensing Act of 1737 which afflicted the whole future of the English stage with a restriction upon its freedom of speech. In the nineteenth and twentieth centuries commercialism has laid a grasping hand upon the stage.

In the Elizabethan age the drama had the patronage of the Court even when it had to struggle against the Puritan authorities. It contrived, in its earlier periods at least, to be a genuinely national drama appealing to all classes and to men and women at different levels of education and intelligence. The dramatists seemed to remember the mixed audiences which had watched the medieval plays, and it is as if they were determined to serve them while enacting the themes and the high sentiments which the Court enjoyed. Already in the seventeenth century one becomes aware that the courtly element is increasing, the writers such as Beaumont and Fletcher are consciously superior to the citizens, whom Dekker and Shakespeare treated with such good-humoured tolerance. The conditions of the Elizabethan theatre lay midway between medievalism and the modern age, and this, assisted by a genuine national consciousness so valuable to the dramatist and the happy accident of the presence of men of genius, made the end of the sixteenth century and the beginning of the seventeenth the greatest age in the English theatre.

It would not be useful in this brief record to particularize on the merits of the individual dramatists of the period. English, American and Continental scholarship has performed one of its greatest services in its minute study of the meagre record of their lives and the corrupt text of their plays. Indeed it might well be urged that in England these plays have been studied too often and seen too seldom. England now requires a cycle of State-aided theatres in which the plays of this and other periods can be performed without the anxieties and uncertainties of commercial management. Such a theatre would naturally encourage new work, but an audience that was aware of its past in drama would be the one best prepared to welcome the newcomer. Much in the poetic drama of the Elizabethan age would still find a response amid modern audiences. The plots of Christopher Marlowe might now seem ineffective, but the majesty of the verse, which seeks the uttermost bounds of human knowledge for its comparisons, would make *Tamburlaine* and *Dr Faustus* still acceptable. Ben Jonson has already found willing audiences in the twentieth century, though he is still too over-shadowed by Shakespeare's reputation. The figure of Volpone is one of universal application, and Jonson's picture of man's weaknesses and humours, though rendered somewhat grim by the pathological element in his comedy, makes him the great social dramatist of the English stage. The later drama of the Jacobean and Carolean age has still the power to appeal, though often its motives are more intricate and the personalities portrayed more corrupt. John Webster, in both *The White Devil* and *The Duchess of Malfi*, has been able to reach modern audiences by the poetical portrayal of a world pitiless in its cruelty. Even Dekker with his merry and romantic picture of citizen life in *The Shoemaker's Holiday* or Cyril Tourneur in the monstrous and sensual world of *The Revenger's Tragedy* and *The Atheist's Tragedy* is still intelligible to audiences today. Much in the drama of that time is dross, the stale imitation of genius, but much else is permanently effective, and the encouragement of the production of these old masters in our own age is a welcome development in the modern English theatre.

No drama can, however, live on the splendours of a single period. The drama must be a living drama refashioned from one age to another. The English drama is a living drama, though it is difficult to discover the same developing tradition as in fiction or poetry. The dramatist is more dependent than the poet or the novelist on immediate financial support, on social conditions and on the national reputation of his art. It must be admitted that the long-continued Puritan hostility combined with censorship and commercialism have made the task of the dramatist in England one of considerable difficulty. During the period of the Commonwealth, 1649-60, the theatres were closed, and though superficially the dramatists of the Restoration seem to continue the old tradition, actually the break had been a deep one separating the drama from the life of the people. The best in the drama of the Restoration period was to be found in the comedy of Wycherley and Congreve, whose brilliant and amoral picture of elegant life delighted courtly audiences. Their plays still survive by their wit and belong to the permanent repertoire of the English stage.

The eighteenth century has little in its drama to match its great achievement in poetry, fiction and philosophy. Walpole's Licensing Act drove many good men, including Henry Fielding, out of drama into other forms of literary activity. Nor can it be denied that the rising middle classes could give little encouragement to dramatists: the audiences were content with mediocrity and too often obtained it. In compensation there were some outstanding exceptions. John Gay in 1728 composed *The Beggar's Opera*, the lyrics and burlesque of which have a liveliness that attracts modern audiences, even though they may be uninstructed in the topical satire of Walpole which the piece so cunningly contains. Oliver Goldsmith produced in 1773 *She Stoops to Conquer*, a comedy which English audiences have always enjoyed. Its plot is wildly improbable, but it has a genial interest in comic characterization to which the English have always made a generous response. A few years later Richard Sheridan wrote two comedies, *The Rivals* and *The School for Scandal*, which revive something of the wit of the

Restoration plays without indulging in their immoralities. Sheridan had not the unique vision which Jonson possessed, but he portrayed his age in themes which any age can understand.

Much of the drama of the nineteenth century in England is distressingly poor. There were no large elements in the community ready to treasure the drama as an art. Commercialism laid its ugly hands more heavily upon the nation, and the masters of industry considered the drama, when they considered it at all, as the play-time occupation of their hours of leisure. If drama were to revive it would have to do so by exposing the conditions which were attempting to destroy it. The importance of a play such as T. W. Robertson's *Caste*, despite all its crudities and inadequacy, was that it was moving in the right direction, for it was a genuine and satirical picture of society. The same conditions prevailed in other European countries and it would be a corrective to any excessive commendation of this play to recall that Ibsen's *Peer Gynt* was produced in the same year of 1867.

In the twentieth century the drama has revived in a most promising way, and given possible conditions, which I think must include some State aid in production, it has a reasonable prospect after the war. Every type of drama has contributed to the revival. Comedy has had a varied career, from the brief brilliance of Oscar Wilde in the eighteen-nineties to the long career of G. B. Shaw, who wrote plays for over half a century. He made the drama the servant of ideas, and his ideas have covered all the conceivable problems of theology, politics and morals. The service which he thus performed to a theatre that was barren of ideas is enormous. One may register the single regret that his genius did not lead to a drama that would make more distinct calls on the actor's art or on the skill of a scenic designer. Too often he relied on his own brilliant rhetoric to hold the audience and he reduced the actor from being the master of dialogue and gesture to the role of a speech-maker.

Shaw's pre-eminence may give comedy a foremost place in the modern theatre; and in the record of comedy such plays as J. M. Synge's *The Playboy of the Western World* and Sean O'Casey's *Juno and the Paycock* have further increased the great debt which England owes Ireland. Apart from comedy the modern stage has seen the notable revival of poetic drama, varying from *The Countess Cathleen* of W. B. Yeats, in which the poetry seemed to have become somewhat detached from the drama, to *Murder in the Cathedral* by T. S. Eliot, where poetry and drama are brought back to the united purpose which they possessed in the Elizabethan age. Nor is the revival in drama confined to the few names which I have mentioned. Sir James Barrie, John Galsworthy, St. John Ervine, J. B. Priestley, Christopher Fry and a number of others have produced work which can compare favourably with that of any dramatist in the nineteenth century, and with that of all but some three dramatists of the eighteenth century.

XVIII

LITERATURE'S place is probably shifting in an age of mass media, and yet it is upon literature that culture will depend. Culture, employed as I now employ it, to include thought, creation and the practice of the arts, must develop an entirely new conception if life is to develop. Civilized man must realize that the material and economic aspects of existence are only preliminaries to make the cultural life possible. One must look forward to a far more liberal interchange between countries of the arts, music, pictures and literature in all its forms. The curse of Babel will still pursue literature, but translation can do much more than it has so far been allowed to achieve. That interchange is ultimately a glorification of life which no diplomatic and political interchange can ever attain. The alternatives that lie before civilized man are either this large and enriched life or a new and more dreadful barbarism. In that interchange England can receive much, but she has also much to offer.

INDEX